Raised by Wolves

The Darkness Before the
Elizabeth Smart Abduction

By

Derrick L. Thompson

authorHOUSE™

1663 LIBERTY DRIVE, SUITE 200
BLOOMINGTON, INDIANA 47403
(800) 839-8640
WWW.AUTHORHOUSE.COM

First published by AuthorHouse 02/15/05

ISBN: 1-4208-3443-6 (sc)

Printed in the United States of America
Bloomington, Indiana

This book is printed on acid-free paper.

DEDICATED TO:

My son, Andrew, your arrival brought me hope for a new beginning.

My sister, LouRee, your unconditional love helped me discover my true self.

INTRODUCTION:

How do I introduce this book or myself? To start, my parents are not good people. The life my siblings and I endured with them is loaded with pitfalls. From conception, birth and lives beyond, we are cursed. Thanks to our parents' lack of the ability to parent, we were their victims, and the people who would become involved with our lives became victims as well.

With that said, I will tell you my childhood was not pleasant. My parents projected a lot of their "garbage" on to me, subsequently; I applied it to my life. My name is Derrick Thompson, and my mother, Wanda Barzee is in a mental institution for her role in the Elizabeth Smart kidnapping. Many of you know the Smart's side of the story, but have yet to hear how this dramatic event has affected those on the other side of it, both before and after the kidnapping.

This is the story of my life, and it involves many players and memories I find misfortunate to have recalled over my short thirty-five year life. I have changed most names to protect myself, but the story is the same.

Our family is "good-sized" by Mormon standards. I am the middle child out of six children, or the fourth one born from two psychotic parents. I guess my point is; being the fourth in-line, has afforded me the opportunity to recall the gauntlet of abuse suffered by myself, as well as the older and younger siblings in my family. Now, other members of the community have suffered from the abuse as well.

I am glad Elizabeth was found safe and returned home. I even feel a sense of pride in knowing I helped get her home, but her tragic nine-month ordeal, in my opinion, is a small taste of the many years I served with my mother, my father, and Brian Mitchell, as well as my understanding of the Mormon faith.

Please read with an open mind, as I do not look kindly upon the Mormon faith. Truthfully, I feel that I could have been raised in any religion-based home rather than Mormon and come out with bitterness toward that religion, but it happened to be the Mormon religion in my case. Do not get me wrong, like several Christian-based religions; the Mormons have certain family values that are good for the people involved and the communities they reside. However, we as humans are not perfect, nor will we ever be, and the typical Mormon attitude, I've learned, is that Mormons are perfect and can do no wrong. My book is filled with many things "outstanding" Mormons did, and continue to do, very wrong.

From a young age, I feel that I've had the ability to see through bullshit, and my perspective has guided me to write this book. I am not an English major and, as I discovered, books are hard for me to write, but this writing has helped with my personal well-being. I hope this book may help others who have lived dysfunctional lives; to know there is always opportunity for escape from the darkness. I believe that for my parents, it's too late; my mother's brain is clouded with sickness and Jesus. My father is an abusive man who still lives a very depressing life. As far as the very disturbed Brian Mitchell goes, I wouldn't mind if someone did us all a favor, and wiped him off the Earth.

In a way these people taught me many things. Not directly, but indirectly through my eyes and this life of mine. I will give my parents credit for two things; my conception, I do enjoy life, and helping me find the truth. Through their examples, they showed me what not-to-do.

CHAPTER ONE:
TOO MANY PUPPIES

Lynwood, California: July 21, 1969. In a Catholic hospital north of Compton, my mother gave birth to her fourth child. Derrick Lael Thompson was put on the birth certificate, and I arrived on the earth oblivious to what life had in store for me. I was a towheaded blonde kid with big, blue eyes ready to take whatever life threw at me.

My father, Theodore, or Ted as he liked to be called, was from South Carolina and became a convert to the Mormon Faith around the time he was eighteen. For one reason or another, he found himself in Utah, going to church. He met his future wife, Wanda, at their local church ward where they began their courtship. She was already engaged at the time, but I think her fiancée was on a mission for the Mormon Church and not around. From what I've been told, this did not deter Ted. He eventually won her over and the two became engaged. Their engagement was not long; and Wanda was married at the young age of eighteen to somebody ten years her senior. With that union, the right forces had combined to create a life of pain and suffering for everyone, inside or around this family unit.

Mormons are taught to populate the earth with as many of their own kind as they can, so freshly into her marriage, Wanda was pregnant with my oldest sister, Rachel, and at the young age of nineteen, gave birth to her first child. With a new baby in her arms, my mother was happy and filled with the hope new babies bring. Wanda showed a lot of love to her first child, and they formed an early bond together. When Rachel was about two, my oldest brother, Brad was born, and one day shy of a year, my sister

1

Alicia arrived on the earth bringing the total head count in our family to five.

My father was a student during these times, and my family moved to California so my father could finish his degree. He was wrapping up a Masters Degree in Physical Education and still had a couple of years to go. I don't know if Wanda was pregnant with me at the time of their move or if I was conceived in California, but I do know that I was born within the first year my family was in California. My parents were barely getting by financially at this time, and I believe somebody from my parents' church worked at the Catholic hospital, and this person informed someone of importance at the hospital of my family's money situation, and the hospital let me come into the world - free of charge. Being the first and only child in my family "born free," gave me a pretty good start receiving attention from my parents. I remember my father mentioning it all the time when I was very young, and I enjoyed hearing him tell the story of my free birth.

From the Hospital, I was taken home to meet my new family. I took up residence where we all lived in a small apartment in Anaheim while my dad finished school. Two years later Ted received his degree, and my first of many moves took place. I have always referred to this move as our "Mormon migration". Ted could have made more money with his education in California, but he and Wanda wanted to live in the "promised land" so off to Hunter, Utah we went. Almost as soon as we arrived in Hunter, my youngest brother, Kelly, was born. This brought the head count of our family to seven, and my mother was barely in her mid-twenties.

The kindness and love my older siblings had been experiencing from their mother was fading with the arrival of each new child. The more children that Wanda gave birth to, the farther she would detach from all of the children. Mormons, from what I understand, are usually married at very young ages and give birth to several children in a short amount of time. Some young women can cope with this very well, others cannot. I feel that Wanda was one of those people whom could not handle this new life that was thrust upon her. My mother's mental state was, probably, somewhat normal back when her first three children were born, however, my mother is a very selfish person by nature, and the more Ted impregnated her, the more she detached from her family. My mother's mental condition was starting to be put to the test and her grades as a mother were bound to get worse.

2

My first memories of life started in Hunter. I vaguely remember my early childhood; up until the age of four, or so. What I can tell you is that some of these early memories are of my parents being very happy, and we children well loved. These memories quickly change for me as my mother's mental health starts to deteriorate. At the tender age of four, I made my way into my parents' room where I observed my mother crying uncontrollably. I had no idea why she was crying, and it terrified me.

"What's wrong mommy?" I remember asking her.

"Get out of here Derrick; you don't need to see me like this," she said.

I was very afraid for her and wanted to help her, but I did not know how. "What made her sad like this?" I wondered. She looked like a child younger than myself crying for help, and I found myself less scared and more curious the longer I watched her.

After staring at her for a few minutes, I backed out of my parents' room and closed the door. Being this young, I had no understanding of what was wrong with my mother. I recall overhearing my dad talking to my older siblings, "Your mother needs some medicine because the chemicals in her head are unbalanced." I would often hear the phrase "mental health," and I did not know what it referred to, but it was scary to me as a child, so naturally I feared for my mother. With Wanda being severely bi-polar, these crying fits had probably happened before. I just do not recall it before this time.

It was also at this tender age I notice something else; Ted did not like it when our mom would get so emotional, and he thought beating the shit out of her would help snap her out of her depression. I remember times standing petrified, as I watched him slap her around. Beating up Wanda only worked for Ted's temporary well being, and Wanda started to find more comfort at church rather than home. The Mormon Church became a refuge for Wanda, and she spent a lot of time there, both physically and mentally. Wanda was a member of the Mormon Church from her birth, and she always had a great love for God, Jesus and her Faith. My mother learned to read music and play the piano at a very young age. One of her main aspirations was to play music for God, and it still is today.

I remember when my mother received a calling from the church to play the piano each Sunday for our ward house, and my mom was very excited about it. Wanda fit into this position well, and she thrived from the attention it earned her. Every Sunday we would go to church, and all I would hear is how beautiful Wanda's music was, and how people felt the "Holy Ghost" as she played. I was calling it "bullshit" even at this very early age. God, Jesus, or the Holy Ghost, I did not care who they were. I just wanted a mother, and I was angry with God because I felt he was taking my mother from me.

"Why does he need my mom to play for him?" I remember thinking.

Some of my earliest memories are hearing from my parents and from people at my church how much God loved me. I didn't care how much god *supposedly* loved me because I wanted my parents to do that. It was clear to me, early on, that my mom enjoyed her music much more than she enjoyed her children. With Wanda Rocking for God, her motherly duties would decline, and any love for us would be put on hiatus. Wanda has a big smile, and I remember using her smile as a love meter. If our mother was happy, love translated through the ranks, and peace would find a way into our home. When our mother was sad the world would change, and the sound of church music would ring through the house, and Ted would have some spiritual tunes to beat his children to.

We were never really sure when our next beating would come so from early ages we were all pointing fingers and telling lies. Sure, we were told lying was bad, but when you live in fear, it becomes a natural instinct of survival to lie.

POOF! A white cloud of flour engulfs my brother Kelly, covering him from head to toe. I was four years old at the time so that would have put him at about three. I do not remember why I did it, but for some reason I busted a large bag of flour on his head.

"What was that?" bellowed Wanda from atop the stairs.

I figured my brother and I would be killed when our mother came down the stairs and saw the basement looking like a cocaine deal gone bad. On the contrary, in fact, she came down and saw her youngest looking like a graduate from the "Cracka Factory," and she lost it.

"I didn't do it!" I quickly said.

She gave me the "yeah right" look and then saw how funny her youngest appeared with his blue eyes the only distinguishable feature. Wanda

4

laughed uncontrollably for about ten minutes, and then she pulled out the camera and snapped a picture (there is still a photo of that floating around somewhere). That is one of my first memories of my mom laughing, and the first time noticing I could have been a prop-comic. I had to clean up the mess, but Wanda helped me. **I was thrilled by the attention my mom gave me, and I discovered myself doing similar things to get that kind of attention from her.**

Some children naturally have to draw negative attention on themselves in order to feel the love they need. I was one of these children. There were a lot of children running around our house, and there was hardly any love to go around. I remember starving for love and attention. I wanted my parents to notice me at almost any cost. My grabs for the spotlight started out harmless enough; a rock up the nose here, a garbage-bag parachute off the deck there, but I still was not garnishing the results I needed. Sure I would get the occasional laugh, but I needed more.

I think the first words I learned to read were, "Blue Diamond Matches." Fire became my tool of choice to draw more attention to myself, and I learned to use it well. Our neighbors had just built a new cedar fence and I decided to see if, "Strike Anywhere" really meant what it said, and it certainly did. Some tumble weeds had gathered by a corner of the fence begging me to send them to hell. A short rub down the cedar with the match, and I instantly had my own version of the "burning bush," which quickly spread to the fence and destroyed a large portion of it. With that, I received the attention I so desperately needed. Before this incident, I do not remember any *real* beatings I received from my dad, but I definitely remember that one, and there would be plenty more to follow. My dad whipped me with a belt for what seemed like an hour. He did not just focus on my small bottom though; he whipped my back and legs as well. I ended up with blue and red welts all over me. Wanda stood by never saying a word. Whether my mother was afraid for her own safety or she just didn't care, I wasn't sure.

Beatings were all in a days work for my father, and he performed his job well. Ted had the ability to become extremely psychotic at times. I guess the best way to describe him, in my opinion, is a nice guy to everyone at Church, but a complete asshole to his family at home. Some of my first memories of my father are of him whipping one of my siblings or myself into a bloody pulp for some stupid reason or another. At first, his physical control of us mostly consisted of cowhide on the backside. Kelly and I discovered early on that if you put various pairs of underwear on, the belt lashings did not hurt as bad. Sometimes Ted would give us advance warning when he was going to whip us, and we used it to our advantage.

"Go into your room and think about what you did, and I'll be there in a minute," he would say.

The only thing we thought about was protecting our tender asses. We would run to our room, close the door, and head for the underwear drawer. Our little legs jumped through several pair until we felt we had the desired amount on for his level of anger. With three pair, he would probably whip us only a few times concentrating on the buttocks. If we put on anything over five pair, it meant we were probably in for a "big one", and maybe the underwear was not going to save us, but we had to try.

With my father becoming more abusive, and my mother more neglectful, our family and the relationship we had was suffering. Wanda wanted us all to start going to counseling. My father hated this idea. I remember him seeming almost terrified of the whole thing.

"We don't need to waste money on shrinks," I recall him saying.

My father was, obviously not afraid of Wanda physically, but he seemed terrified of the thought of losing her, so with the threat of a divorce, Wanda got what she wanted, and our family started counseling sessions. I was very young at the time (5 or 6), but I still remember wondering why we kids had to be there. It seemed that my parents were always playing these little mind-games, and we children were stuck in the middle of them. Some early conversations about my mother's mental health were from Ted. I remember hearing him talk about Wanda having "mood swings", and how she could not control them. When I heard my father give his opinion on her "mood swings" I always questioned them.

"This guy is talking about my mom's moods. What about yours, dad," I would ponder.

I cannot recall exactly how long our counseling lasted, but I know it was not effective. Ted and Wanda knew something was wrong in their lives. They just could not pinpoint it and were blaming each other, so we all had the pleasure of helping them cope through their abuse and neglect.

Early in my life, I began trying the abuse that I was learning from my father. At our parents' friend's house, I remember the people showing us their baby. The child was about a year old. It was in the evening, and the young child was in his crib. After everyone left the room, I made my way back in and looked at the baby. He was still awake and smiled at me as I gazed upon him. I reached my arm through the crib bars and grabbed as much of his thin baby hair as I could. I pulled at his hair hard through the bars to try and make him cry. The tough little guy did not make a peep. He just kept smiling at me so I eventually gave up. I left his room feeling bad about trying to hurt the young child, and to this day, I still feel incredible guilt about it. Children learn behavior very early from their parents and surroundings, and looking back, I know it's why I treated that baby this way.

My dad loves sports, and I think that is why he chose to become a Physical Education Teacher. Ted put his hard-earned Masters Degree to work as a coach at Cottonwood High School. From what I remember, he seemed pretty happy at his job. Ted liked to take us to the basketball games he was coaching and let us "hang out" with him. At these games I noticed how well my dad was treating other people around him. Along with coaching basketball, he also taught Driver's Education at the High School. Ted would let some of us kids ride along as he taught the students how to drive. He was always nice to these people, I recall feeling, as I watched his interactions with them. It started raising a lot of questions in me about whom my father was.

I became very observant of Ted's actions, and I began to evaluate everything he did. I wondered why when it was just his children in the car, he had no problem pulling the vehicle over and beating us into submission. When Ted's students drove with him, they could make several mistakes, but he just encouraged them to do better. For his children at home there was no encouragement, only beatings. He was not showing us the love he showed other people because he was ignorant about who mattered in his life. The people in our Church were also very impressed with Ted because my dad was a completely different person when he was at Church. At home, however, he acted as himself, and I sometimes found him quite amusing to watch. If a sporting event, Ted was interested in, fell on a Sunday, he would still go to Church, but afterward he would be glued in front of the television with his Sunday clothes off and his garments still on. Garments are very sacred to Mormons and are not supposed to be shown to anyone, which is why this amused me. My dad was sitting on the couch, fresh from the holy talk he received at Church, watching the Utah Jazz and cursing at the television.

"You fucking stupid ref, how can you call that a foul?" he would loudly complain.

While Ted watched sports in his Mormon underwear, I learned how to swear with the best of them.

"Goddamn it, when are they going to get rid of that worthless Mark Eaton?" was another line I recall him saying.

"Did my father really like anyone?" I questioned.

The only love I understood from Ted came after he beat us, and he would feel the remorse of his actions. Usually an hour or so after he raged on us, he would show up in our bedroom where we licked our wounds to apologize. After his apathetic apologies, it was off to Dan's supermarket where we would all get ice cream. On birthdays and other present-giving holidays he tried to curb his guilt by buying us a lot of gifts. Christmas became a really good holiday for the Thompson children. Below our Christmas tree, piles of presents were increasingly gaining altitude.

I had a strong belief of Santa Claus, and I loved how he knew what I wanted every year. Sometimes I got things I never even asked for. My siblings helped fuel my beliefs by telling me I had just missed Santa Claus (or the Easter Bunny depending on the Holiday). I had no idea what to think about these God and Jesus guys my mother and father kept talking about. I always saw this Santa guy at the mall, so the evidence seemed indisputable. From racetracks to Star Wars figures we were getting the toys we wanted, but the love was next to nothing.

My mom always mentioned how she could feel and see the "Holy Spirit". I remember it disturbed me. In fact, I would worry about her because her eyes would glaze over, and she would draw a blank look on her face. This look of hers could mostly be seen when she mashed the keys of the organ or piano while she played Christmas music or practiced for Church. **With our mother in a Christ induced coma; it became a game with some of us to try and snap her out of it**. Sneaking up from behind her, my younger brother and I would push the foot pedals with our hands, and throw off any note she was playing at the time. This, of course, would infuriate her, and she would scream how we made the "Spirit" leave the house.

"Good, it bothered me having him around anyway," I remember thinking.

We did a lot of activities when I was young, but one of my favorites was going to an amusement park north of Salt Lake City called Lagoon. We went there often, and we were often left to our own accord. Lagoon, at the time, had a Fun House. This was one of my favorite places to go inside the park. The Fun House had a large metal slide that people would go down in gunnysacks. After maneuvering through the labyrinth of obstacles that made up the Fun House, the big slide was the last thing everyone did before they exited. On this particular day, everything went well as I made my way through the Fun House, until I got to the slide at the end. I grabbed my brown sack and went down the slide. Toward the end of the slide, I fell over sideways and my right eye brushed over a screw that was sticking out. My eyelid tore almost completely off, and as I got up people instantly started "freaking out". I remember little, except, somebody rushing me to the First Aid building with blood pouring down my face. My parents were nowhere to be found, and I had to sit there for, what seemed like hours, until Ted was located and could take me to get stitches. I preferred to be away from my parents whenever I could, but I wanted them around when I needed them. **This was one of my earliest memories of wondering if I had parents that cared about any of their children.**

Drama was surrounding us very early on, and most of the causes seemed to be from our parents not knowing where we were at any given time.

"Have any of you kids seen Alicia?" Wanda nervously asked one day.

My sister had been missing for about four hours, and nobody knew where she was. An all-out neighborhood search ensued, and we looked for Alicia. I remember being scared for my sister, but I was still not exactly sure what was going on. With everybody in a panic, and a search in progress, I observed my mom's behavior. I thought she was concerned for her daughter, but since she seemed the most calm out of everyone, I felt she didn't really care.

"What is she going to do, just have another kid if she can't find this one?" I recall thinking.

Alicia was eventually found at the bottom of her bed, sound asleep. During an afternoon nap she worked her way down to the bottom of her bed and was completely hidden by her covers. They checked her bedroom when they began looking for her, but they apparently passed her over. We were all relieved when Alicia was found, and everybody got a laugh out of it. This was life for us early on. Ted and Wanda never cared anything about us until something went wrong.

When I was about five we went to my aunt's house, Wanda's sister Jackie. After a few minutes there, boredom took over and I began to explore her house. I made my way down to the basement where I discovered a locked gun cabinet. Inside the cabinet, I spotted a BB gun, and my little brain decided I needed it. I used something to smash the glass, and the noise went unheard. I stared in awe at the weapons in front of me, but focused mostly on the BB gun. I remember the gun clearly. It was a Daisy Red Rider BB gun. Kelly and I were never apart for very long, and he showed up in the basement shortly after I removed the gun from the cabinet. Upon seeing my brother, a stupid idea entered my head to test the weapon on him. He did not go for the idea of me shooting him, and instead of wasting my time trying to talk Kelly into it, I pinned him to the ground, holding his arms with my legs. He was four at the time so it was quite easy for me to force him down and hold the gun barrel to his tiny chest. While he was subdued, I cocked the lever, pulled the trigger, and "POP" the BB ripped through his shirt and embedded into his skin at the center of his sternum. Kelly instantly screamed in pain, and then sprinted up the stairs to warn everyone of the five-year-old psychopath he had encountered.

I cannot clearly remember why I did this to him. The only thoughts I recall are of me wanting to try a BB gun, and how determined I was to do so. I was punished for committing this act and remember Wanda lecturing me while she pulled up my brother's shirt and showed me the small scab that formed on his chest. My aunt and uncle were also upset with me, and I could no longer go anywhere in their house without some kind of supervision until I was a few years older. At least, somebody knew what we needed; too bad it wasn't my parents. Other than that one incident, I loved going to my relatives' homes as a child. My siblings and I were always well received by them, and all of our cousins got along great with us. Most of the people on Wanda's side of the family are Mormon, with a few exceptions. My cousins all seemed well loved and very happy, die-hard Mormons or not. **I guess love promotes harmony, and I was envious of my cousins and their happy families.**

Grandma and grandpa's house, on Wanda's side, was by far my favorite place to go as a child. My grandmother loved to cook and we always had good, home-cooked meals when we went to see them. My grandfather, Gary was always glad to see us, and he had unique talents. Gary was actually my step-grandfather, due to my biological grandfather's death from lung cancer when I was two. One of Gary's talents was playing the saw. Using a violin bow, he would bend the saw on his leg then run the bow over the non-business end of the saw. He was quite talented with it and could play almost any song we requested. Sometimes he would enlist the help from one of those old-school toy monkeys that played the symbols, smacked his lips, and rolled his eyes around. My grandpa and that monkey would jam for hours, keeping everybody entertained. I learned a lot from my Grandpa Gary and wished my dad were kind and loving like him. Gary also polished rocks and made old cowboy jewelry from the shiny stones. I enjoyed my grandpa's talents and thrived from the unconditional love he showed me. I did not experience that kind of genuine love at home, and I found myself starting to crave it. I grew resentful that I could not live with a loving family like my relatives seemed to have. I would find comfort and love at our relatives' homes any chance I could, and I would act out around my parents because of the resentment I felt toward them. I would think, "We should be more like these families, and not the way we are." Why couldn't my parents see this? As far as I was concerned, everything my parents were teaching their children was a lie.

My feelings started culminating a deep resentment for the Church I was supposed to believe in, as well as toward the parents I was supposed to trust. My Grandpa and Grandma were devout Mormons, and they would talk about their faith all the time, but it was always questionable to me. I looked outwardly at the other families in my life, and it seemed they were practicing what they preached, but it wasn't genuine where it counted for me, at home.

Around the tender age of six, Ted's weapon of choice became his bare hands. The belt was put away, and in its place were his fists. My true feelings toward my father presented themselves as he beat my younger brother and me. With his fists in full fury, and our bedroom walls his sadistic boundary, Ted was beating the life out of us. After punching me in the face several times, he threw Kelly against the wall and started in on him.

I stepped back and screamed at him, "You're a child abuser!" "You're supposed to be kind and love us, but all you do is beat us up." "You're going to Hell!"

Well, for that particular moment, calling my *Mormon* father a child abuser, and telling him he's going to Hell made him stop to evaluate the situation. He quit hitting us and left the room. I always hated the fact that all this abuse was happening under God's nose, and he was not doing anything about it. My prayers as a child consisted of me asking for answers from God. I knew the story of the Mormon Prophet, Joseph Smith, and how he prayed to get his questions answered, and God answered them. I put everything into my prayers and expected to hear from God, personally. Sometimes at night I cried, begging God to make my parents good to us. Of course, my prayers were not answered, and my faith in God was repeatedly questioned.

Church became a big waste of time for me, and I was still just a small boy. I would see other children, even some of my friends, who were very strong in their faith and stood convinced that everybody was speaking the truth. This feeling was hogwash to me, and I always felt like an outsider for it. In Sunday school I was less interested in the teachings and more content on acting like a clown. Sacrament meeting was usually the first place we went as followers of the faith. It consisted of all the members in that particular ward to meet in the main room of the Church, listen to the elders speak, and sing songs of faith passed on through generations of Mormons. It mostly meant a good nap for me. With a sandwich bag of Cheerios and a place to rest, I could usually sleep through the torture.

Mormons fast one Sunday a month, so we could count on not eating all that day until dinnertime. It was the worst for me at Church on Fast Sunday. Members of the church would stand up, grab a microphone and bear their testimony to the "one true religion". To bear one's testimony means to confirm their choice of the right faith to the entire congregation, and then tell a short story about something that happened in their lives and how God helped them out. Children are encouraged to bear their testimonies, and they would form a long line to have their turn. They repeated each other over and over until the microphone passed through the entire line. Ted and Wanda would get up and bear their testimonies once in a while, and I, so badly, wanted to scream and call them liars.

I think as my father started making more money, my parents were convinced the grass would be greener in Sandy, Utah. I was about six when I heard we were going to move. With our house in Sandy being built, our time in Hunter drew to a close. Before the house was completed, my family took a short, fifteen-minute drive, to Sandy to look at our new home. The contrast between the two houses was incredible for me. Our old house was complete "white trash" compared to our new home. The flaking paint on the exterior wood and the dead lawn are the main things that stood out to me of our old house. The new home in Sandy was a dark red, brick house over 3,000 square feet inside with a big front yard that steeped downhill with railroad ties and fern terraces. In Ted and Wanda's bedroom there was an entrance to a giant, covered patio that sat on top of the equally big garage. It appeared to be middle class heaven.

"Things will be great from now on," I remember thinking.

If memory serves me correctly, the move went off without a hitch, and we arrived at our new Sandy paradise. We established ourselves in the local ward and before she knew it, Wanda played the organ for the church again. Our new neighbors were pretty cool, and the lady that lived across the street from us had a son who was a television star. His name was Johnny Whitaker, and he was the red headed kid in one of my favorite shows at the time, "Sigmund and the Sea Monsters." He was in town one time when we were new in our church ward, and his mother gave me an autographed picture of him at church.

"COOL" I thought. "We just moved in where Movie Stars live. This has to be the greatest house ever!"

Our home was on a dead-end street next to a big, sagebrush field, a large gravel pit, and a golf course with plenty of water. Everything that neglected children need to get themselves killed was all around us, and I took advantage of every opportunity. The golf course was just down the hill from our home with a small pond and a small creek on it. My sister, Alicia, and I were hanging out on the golf course, throwing rocks into the creek. The creek was not large, about three feet across, but at times the water was quick. Without paying attention, I slipped into the swift moving water. I was too small to do anything except ride the current on the log just formed in my little pants. Alicia was magnificent at protecting me and sprinted down the creek's edge until she reached a spot to pull me out.

"Don't ever do that again, Derrick!" she sternly told me.

I concurred, and we decided the creek was not the best spot for us to hang out. We still loved the golf course though, and all of us children found several activities to do there.

I was always hatching half-baked schemes to satisfy my young creativity. With a piece of plywood, some nails, and an old tractor seat, I fabricated what I thought would be a great boat to float on the pond. Kelly and I hauled the makeshift boat the quarter mile or so to the pond and sat it in the water. I was confident in my design and was determined to go first. I walked to the edge of the pond and jumped on the board landing in the seat. My momentum and weight flipped me off the worthless boat, and all of a sudden my world was dark and wet. I did not know how to swim, but managed to "doggy paddle" my way to shore and safely crawl out of the water. We left that stupid boat at the pond, and I went home soaking wet. Wanda found out what we were trying to accomplish and yelled at us.

Just a few hours after I survived the pond incident, some bad news spread through the neighborhood about a boy drowning in that same pond. Everybody near the general area gathered around the pond to see the rescue crew at work. The pond was small, maybe thirty feet across by sixty feet long, but it was fifteen feet or more deep, and it had a young boy trapped in it's murky depths. He, along with some of his friends, was playing on a log when he slipped off and hit his head. The boy's father was at the scene, desperately hoping it would not be his child that was pulled from the pond. The boy was under water for about an hour before I got there, and it took another hour for him to be found. Suddenly the rescue workers yelled out, "We got him, we got him" and their small boat was quickly pulled to shore with the boy's lifeless body hanging out the back. I looked over as the boy's father saw his child blue and void of life. He, instantly, fell to the ground screaming, and everybody surrounded him. I stared in awe at this father screaming for his son. **I remember doubting if my father would react with, even the slightest bit of grief if it were my body being pulled from the pond.**

Once again, I had the feeling that my parents loved their children less by the day, and the older we grew, the less they cared about us as well.

CHAPTER TWO:
WEANED

When Christmas came in our new home, I awoke to find a shiny bicycle under the tree. Kelly usually got the same things I got every year because of our closeness in age. That year Santa gave my brother a bike as well, and we both loved our new bikes. I don't think Santa's Elves made helmets, though, because we never got one of those.

When we lived in Hunter, my older brother, Brad, taught me to ride a bike, and I picked up the activity rapidly. Sandy was a great city for a kid with a bike; it was a new development so there were a lot of hills and dirt all around us. We became very independent on our bikes and rode them all over. Kelly and I loved to pretend to be stunt men on our bicycles. At six and seven years old we built bicycle jumps that spanned six-foot wide desert washes. At the end of our street the sidewalk ended, and a small gap formed from erosion. We built a jump using some old plywood, and I prepared to jump it. Me being the older brother, I was usually the first to attempt a stunt, and I knew I needed speed to clear the wash so my little legs pumped the pedals feverishly. I reached the jump with plenty of speed and way too much gusto. My arms jerked back on the handlebars, and I flew like a bird. I cleared the wash by several feet, but managed to lose the bicycle and land square on my back, instantly knocking the air right out of me. This was the first time I had experienced having the wind knocked out of me so I thought I was going to die. I could not breathe. My body squirmed on the ground, while I began to panic. Kelly did not know what to do for me, but Alicia happened to notice my failed attempt at glory and came to my rescue. Alicia picked me up, and she helped me breathe again while reassuring me I would be all right.

Looking back, I feel very grateful to my older siblings; I might not have made it this far without them. Our parents were scarce, and even when we could find them; they seemed not to care about our well-being.

Our home was now big enough to support animal life so one day Wanda made the decision to get us a dog. My mom liked Spaniels, and after she looked in the pet section of the newspaper, she found some Springer Spaniel pups that were ready to find a good home; I said "good home" so I can only hope the other dogs went to one. Wanda picked out a beautiful strawberry-red and white puppy, she wrote a check for the animal and we took her home. Someone thought of the name "Peaches," and we all decided that would be a good name for her. We had our first family pet, and we all enjoyed her. She was a great addition to our family, and we loved the dog very much.

I think that Peaches lived with us for about eight months. Kelly and I were in the bathtub, playing more than we were cleaning, when our mom came in and gave us some bad news.

"Peaches is dead," Wanda said sadly.

We stopped goofing around and both turned to our mother. Our happiness instantly changed to sadness, and I asked my mom "What happened?"

"Your father was backing out of the driveway, and he ran her over," she said.

Kelly and I broke into tears, joining our mother as she wept. It was troubling for all of us, but it must have been the worst for our dad, since he felt responsible for her death. When Ted backed over Peaches, it broke her spine, and he had to rush her to the Vet. She yelped in pain the whole way. There was nothing they could do for Peaches so Ted had her put to sleep and out of her misery. We all missed her companionship, but it was not long before we got another dog.

This dog was an AKC registered English Spaniel. We got her for a good deal because her markings were not "show quality". I think it was my sister, Rachel that gave our new dog her name, Natasha. Natasha was a beautiful dog and very friendly so we bonded quickly with her. During the warm summer evenings, my siblings and I would sleep on our front lawn in sleeping bags. Natasha was right there with us, and she had her choice of whom she would sleep with. She always chose me by crawling into my sleeping bag. She would go to the bottom of my sleeping bag, turn around, and come back up to cuddle with me. Natasha would not do this with anyone else. I always woke up with my nose and mouth full of dog hair, but I did not mind. Natasha and I became very close, and even though she was our family pet, I always thought of her as my dog. We did almost everything together, and I valued her trust and friendship. I became fascinated by her loyalty, and I wondered why my parents were not loyal to me. **I was confused as to why an animal could love me and my mom and dad could not.**

One day, one of our neighbors was cleaning out his garage. He decided to let my brothers, my sisters, and me have first grabs at the goods. We all chose several things from the "free" garage sale. I got an old pair of skis and ski boots. I thought it was great, but I needed some snow. As soon as winter came, I practiced skiing in the field at the side of our house. A forty-foot slope ran down through the sagebrush, and a little snow gave us the perfect sled run or a small ski hill. I practiced on the hill and figured I perfected the ancient wooden skis because I could go down the hill fairly straight, without falling on my ass.

Every year when winter came to Utah, our family found somewhere to go sledding. This particular year, Ted took us to the mountains to go tubing. Ted dropped me off at Alta Ski Resort so I could ski the free "Bunny Hill" while everyone else went tubing. After reaching the Resort, I said goodbye to everyone, and they went back down the canyon to ride their tubes. I stayed behind to ski by myself.

After I went down a couple of runs, my confidence built, and I decided to make a ski jump so I could "show off" for some young girls that had their eyes on me. I built the ski jump by piling up snow and forming it with my hands. When I finished building my jump, I skied to the bottom of the hill and grabbed the tow-rope that pulled me back to the top of the hill. At the top, I waited for the moment the girls were watching. I looked in their direction, and when they looked over at me, I turned to face the jump. When the girls realized my intentions, I leaned my weight forward and headed for the jump. Just before I reached the jump, I looked back to see if they were still watching, and they were. Before I could turn back around, my right ski slipped in a small rut, and I lost control. I crashed as

I went over the jump, and the old wooden ski broke under the pressure. I instantly felt the stupidity of my actions, but that was soon replaced with a severe pain in my right ankle. The girls laughed at me as I grabbed the one good ski and crawled up the hill. Now, I was alone and could not stand on my leg without severe pain. I crawled to a chair, and waited in complete agony for, at least, a couple of hours until my family arrived to get me. I was just a young boy, but I did not look for anyone to help me. When my family finally arrived for me, my tears of pain turned into a flood of joy. They rescued me from the mountain and took me to the Hospital. I had my leg X-rayed, and the X-ray proved my leg was broken, and that my parents were neglectful to have let a small boy ski by himself.

After living in Sandy for a year or so, my baby sister, LouRee came into the world, and she brought the final headcount in our family to eight. With a new baby girl in her arms, Wanda tried to focus her attention on her children again. LouRee was a beautiful little baby, and, from what I could tell at the time, our mom really loved her. I am almost seven years older than my baby sister, and I remember we all took turns taking care of her. I learned how to change nasty cloth diapers and spoon mashed carrots with the best of them. Wanda breastfed the baby, and sometimes I would watch them with envy because of their relationship and the closeness they shared. At times Wanda showed love toward the rest of her children, but that was not often.

My mom was a great cook. She acquired this talent from her mother. It was not just her cooking though; she could bake as well. When she would bake, our big home filled with the smell of irresistible breads and pastries. I recall the aroma of fresh bread making it's way to my bedroom, gently grabbing me by the nose, and guiding me to my mother where we would share a hot slice of bread smothered in butter. We would talk for a while, and she seemed genuinely concerned about me during this time. We did some fun activities in the kitchen with our mom, and one of my favorite things was making suckers. These good memories were fleeting as we grew up because it felt like my mother would select which of her children she wanted to favor, and which of us she would neglect. From about eight years old I remember her love for us was hit or miss. **While my father was physically abusive, Wanda was mentally abusive.**

Because I lacked parental affection, I started to ask my dad what I thought were relevant questions. One time Ted was standing at the kitchen sink rinsing off plates, and I curiously asked him, "Why don't you ever kiss us dad?"

"Do you want me to kiss you?" He replied back.

I felt a little embarrassed then so I asked a different question,

"Shouldn't you, at least, hug us?" I asked quietly.

I do not recall what his reply was, but I do remember feeling odd about asking the questions. With neither parent showing their children much love, or just selective love, from my perspective, I felt alone and very confused.

I always wanted to be bigger so I could defend myself against Ted. I remember thinking if I were a giant, my father would not hurt me. I discovered that when I lifted rocks above my head, the little blue veins in my biceps would pop out. I thought it was the neatest thing to go in the back yard, grab the biggest rock I could hold, and lift it. After lifting the rock a few times, I would run into the bathroom and look in the mirror to see the veins popping out of my arms. I wanted my dad to notice my bulging muscles and to be terrified to hit me. My brother, Kelly noticed my bulging arms instead and began teasing me. Siblings know how to get under each other's skin better than anyone, and this was no exception for Kelly and me. When our dad got upset, he grew the look of a madman, and this look, unfortunately, was passed to his children. When Kelly would piss me off, I would get that look and chase him down.

"Mom, a Mafia Man is after me!" He would scream as he ran to our mother. He called me "Mafia Man" for a short while, and I absolutely hated it. Kelly teased me relentlessly with his new nickname for me so one day I decided to teach him a lesson. I decided, for my entertainment pleasure, our clothes dryer could be a makeshift ride. I went to my brother with the idea that the dryer would be fun to ride if he was only in there for a few seconds. He agreed and crawled inside it. I turned on the dryer for about five seconds, and Kelly appeared to have fun tumbling inside the dryer. I took a ride next while Kelly worked the dryer. A few seconds later, I exited the dryer and told my brother it was his turn again. This was the moment I waited for, and I took full advantage of it. Kelly got back in the dryer, and as soon as he was in there, I placed my weight against the door and turned on the machine. I let the dryer run for about 30 seconds until I heard my brother screaming to get out. When I let him out, he was upset with me.

We got in a fight and he ran to our mother to tell her what the "Mafia Man" did to him.

Kelly did not like his name, because everybody would tease him about it. "Smelly Kelly" was the name most popular with the local kids. One of his friends in the neighborhood was named Richard, and, by coincidence, it is my brother's middle name. Kelly asked that people call him Richard, and his name was changed when he was about six or so. Unfortunately, "Mafia Man" stuck with me for a while longer.

Incest became a part of our lives largely due to us being the unsupervised children we were. One day, Richard and I were approached by two of our older siblings. They wanted us to play "house" with them, and we did. The four of us started having sex in our bedroom closets, with full penetration. I did not have a clue about what I was doing, but they (Brad and Alicia) helped Richard and I figure it out. There was one time when my two brothers and I were in my bedroom having premature sex with our sister, and Rachel walked in and caught us. She immediately ran to Ted and Wanda to tell them what we were doing. I was terrified that I would get my ass kicked, but all my parents did was yell at us and tell us it was not right. Our sexual activity went on for several weeks, until Alicia felt guilty and stopped allowing it. Although my sister stopped the activity, Brad did not. One afternoon he approached me, and with some persistence, Brad talked me into letting him pleasure me orally. I felt uncomfortable about it, but did not know how to express my uneasiness. I did ask him what I was supposed to do, and he said, "Just don't pee in my mouth." I was young, but I still understood this was my way out of it. When he put his mouth on my penis, I released all the urine inside of me. My brother was instantly grossed-out, and he left my room to brush his teeth, I figured. After that, the incest stopped as far as I knew.

Richard and I befriended some kids in the neighborhood who were almost as neglected as we were. Their father was a racecar driver. He met his fate when he crashed his car, and a blood clot formed in his brain. Their mother worked during the day, and she could not afford childcare. Sometimes a babysitter would tend to our friends, but that was not often. One of the babysitters that watched them would lie on the couch, pretending to be asleep, and let us fondle her entire body. She was fourteen, and we were half her age, but she appeared to enjoy the attention. One day Richard and I were over at our friend's house unsupervised, and I discovered something better than any match, a BIC lighter. I started with a simple project by lighting a fire under the kitchen sink. I found a plastic container with a rag in it, and set it on fire. I closed the cupboard door and joined the other children in the living room and watched the television. A few seconds later, Richard noticed smoke coming from the kitchen, and ran to investigate. He acted swiftly, opening the cupboard door, grabbing the container, and rushing it outside. Then Richard turned on the hose, and extinguished the fire on their front lawn. When he came back inside he was baffled.

"How did that happen?" Richard questioned. Everybody was confused as to the fires origin, except for me.

Foiled by Richard at my first project, I decided to try another fire in a different location. I walked into a bedroom at the end of the hallway, opened the closet, and saw a paper bag full of clothes. With one flick of the lighter, I lit the bottom corner of the bag, shut the closet door, and went back to the living room. After a minute or so, black smoke billowed down the hallway. Luckily, everybody was in the living room watching cartoons. We all panicked and ran outside. The fire department was called by one of our neighbors, and the fire was extinguished before the house was completely destroyed.

Right away the Firemen knew it was arson and began interrogating us. The interviews included them smelling our hands to see if they smelled like smoke. Because I used a lighter, my hands were free of smoke odor. My poor brother's hands smelled of smoke because of the fire he had extinguished earlier in the kitchen, and the fire was pinned on him. He, of course, pled his innocence, but nobody believed him (except for me), and since I was an eight-year old chicken shit, I kept to myself and let my brother suffer for it. My dad laid waist to his six-year old son until he confessed to the crime he didn't commit. Although I was ashamed for what had happened that day, I lived with my guilt and kept silent about it until Richard was in his late teens.

Our home was not a pleasant place to be. With our mom neglecting us during the day, it afforded us the opportunity to gain her attention all the wrong ways. When the day was through, Ted would come home and hear about the things we did wrong that day, and then he would proceed to teach us a lesson. He was an abusive tornado ripping its way through our house. And the blood and welts on our small bodies were his indication that he did his job well, as a father. Richard and I started spending a lot of time outdoors to try to dodge the abuse. A year after we got our bikes for Christmas, St Nick gave us each a BB gun. My brother and I became sharpshooters with the weapons and used the guns unsupervised. We had at least three friends with similar weapons, and one time we thought it would be fun to have a BB gun war (as we affectionately called it), and at the side of our house the battle began. Jim, the oldest, had a high-powered pellet gun that could have caused serious injury to any one of us so, we figured for safeties sake, and because the rest of us had low-powered guns that could not shoot as far, he could only put one pump of air in his gun. The war started out okay; we all kept far enough apart from one another because nobody really wanted to get hit, but that changed when Jim stepped off the patio and was hit with a BB in the corner of his eye. Jim instantly screamed in pain, covered his eye with one hand, and threw his gun. Since I was not the one who shot him, I felt safe to go look at his injury. In the corner of his left eye I saw the indentation from the BB about a quarter inch from his eyeball.

"That was a close call," I needlessly said.

Jim calmed down after a couple of minutes, and everyone decided the war was over. We stopped the BB gun battles, but continued to use our weapons in other ways.

Our guns went everywhere with Richard and I, and that was usually in the large sagebrush field by our house. One day while escaping the turmoil in our house, Richard and I headed to the field, and ran into our good friend Jim and his cousin. They had a big German Shepard at their side, and they were burning a small fire. Over the flames, I noticed a stick with a small plucked bird cooking on it. I asked what they were doing and hoped to join their adventure.

"Our parents won't let us keep the dog we found, so we ran away," our friend Jim said.

I found it fascinating that they were living off the land and thought it would be a great idea. I wanted to know more about the Meadowlark B-B-Q that was taking place in front of my eyes.

"Why are you cooking that bird?" I asked.

"Because we're hungry," Jim said, and suddenly it was clear to me. My brother and I could take our BB guns and start new lives of our own. It was a great revelation to me at the time because if Jim and his cousin could live in the wild, we could certainly do it. We had one up on them when we ran away; we took the extra steps necessary to get to an orchard about a mile from our home. We were thinking, not only did we have plenty of birds to eat; we also had a balanced meal with the fruit from the orchard. Almost every free day we had, we would flee our home and live off the land. We were seven and eight-year old survivalist, escaping our wrecked home. We learned how to clean and cook a variety of birds from Sparrows to Robins. We shot some birds merely out of boredom, but we mostly hunted to live, so that we wouldn't have to eat at the abusive home we had escaped from.

I always shared a bedroom with Richard while growing up, and at one point of our lives, we had a room next to our basement storage room. Sometimes before going to bed, we could hear our dad beating the "be-Jesus" out of our mom, in the storage room next to our bedroom. Two pieces of drywall could not contain the horrible noise we heard coming from there. I never saw the abuse that happened in that room, but my small, sensitive ears could hear it. By the sound, I could imagine what was happening to my mom. Ted would throw her up against the shelves, punch her in the head, pull her hair, etc... We would sit in our bedroom listening to a one sided boxing match, as our mom begged him to stop. It did not stop, however, until it seemed she was unconscious. I recall hearing discussions of my dad winning a "Golden Gloves" boxing title while he was in the military. Forty wins with only one loss or something like that. I imagined his one loss to a man, and the forty wins to women and children, though probably not a true statement, very appropriate thinking to me.

At times, my father would make diminutive attempts at showing he cared about us. On one occasion, he was up making oatmeal before we trudged off to school. My sister, Alicia was in a hurry because she was going to miss her bus. As she rushed out the door, Ted told her to sit down and eat before she left. Stuck; now what does she do? Alicia knew if she missed her bus, she would be in trouble, but if she did not sit and eat his nasty oatmeal, the same fate would befall her. She decided to catch the bus and deal with dad later. Her little legs were in a dead sprint to propel her from the house, but she did not make it past the front yard before turning to see a red-faced man chasing her down. Ted tackled his ten-year old daughter, slapped her around, and then dragged her by the hair to the breakfast table. Alicia was forced to eat her oatmeal and miss the bus. When she finished her breakfast, my father made her walk the mile and a half to school. This was how life was with my father. One minute one of his children could skip out the door trying to get to school, and the next minute they could be getting their ass pummeled. **It was a hell of a way for us to live, and I was sick of it.**

My grandfather on my father's side was an abusive S.O.B (according to Ted), as well as the son he raised. I remember my dad sometimes using his father's behavior as an excuse to relieve the guilt that was built up inside of him from his violence towards us. One story I remember from someone in my family about my grandfather is; my grandfather threw money on the floor, waited for my dad to pick it up, and then kicked him in the head. It's really the only story I recall about Ted's dad, but it was enough for me to not want to know my grandfather. We hardly ever visited that grumpy old man. The few times we did go over there, we didn't stay long and didn't say much to him. He ended up dying, alone, in an Old Folks Home, and his funeral was quite sublime. Ted's mother died when he was young due to some type of cancer. I never knew my dad's mother and wondered what she was like and what my dad would be like if she had been around for him. I did not hear much about my grandmother from him, but I could tell he loved and missed her.

Even though our family was in complete disarray, we managed to share several activities. From camping to Church functions, we found ourselves in a lot of different places. I always had the most fun when we went camping, and I had more spiritual experiences camping than I ever had in Church. My distaste for the Mormon Church was established by the time I discovered my passion for camping, and I developed a keen understanding of the people around me. Hypocrisy surrounded me, and it tore apart my faith in the religion I was supposed to believe in. I didn't understand it then, but I knew so many people that were not living like they were to have people believe. I wanted my mom to know my feelings about religion, and for her to see things the way I did so she would love her children more than her church. If I could just make her see things from my perspective, she would leave Jesus in Church and focus on us again. I needed to show her something concrete. I was just not sure what.

With the entire family piled in our old station wagon, we went on a short trip. It was a two-hour drive to a little town where thousands of Mormons flock for the annual, "Miracle Pageant". This was a fun time; get your blanket and pink popcorn balls and let's party. That sounds silly, but what can I say. The whole concept was suspect for me when I heard about it.

"We're going where, to see what?" I remember asking.

I was only nine at the time, and it sounded stupid to me. I did not want to waste a day seeing something I didn't really believe in so making the journey southward to Manti, Utah with eight passengers in our "piece of crap" car seemed unnecessary to me. My mom and dad thought differently though; and everyone else was content with the whole thing. "The Miracle Pageant" is a play about how the Mormon Church came into existence. The story goes that; the Mormon Prophet, Joseph Smith was visited by the Angel Moroni or the "Golden Plate's Fairy," as I think of him. The Golden Plates contained the text of The Book of Mormon, which is what the Mormons live by. These Golden Plates have not been seen, to my knowledge, by anyone other than Joseph Smith.

There we were sitting on a grassy knoll, (where is Lee Harvey when you need him?) watching the Angel float above our hero, Joseph Smith, and I observed the wires that were holding up the holy apparition. As the people sitting around us started their mind- scrubbed banter, my mother started with hers. "Oh, that's so spiritual," she said. I was upset that she believed all of this, and I felt it was my moment to bring her back to Earth. I jumped onto my moms lap, breaking her gaze from the stage with my little hands.

"THE WIRES, CAN'T YOU SEE THE WIRES?!" I adamantly questioned my mother.

As I was screaming at my mother to listen to her nine-year old son, other members of the audience turned to see who was causing the commotion. Wanda did not find humor in this, and my actions garnished immediate results from my father. He smacked me upside the head and dragged me to the car for interrupting this holy event. My mom did not care about the cheesy wires and was overtaken by the fake Angel. My plan failed, and I had to spend the rest of "The Miracle Pageant" in the car where I slept until my Manti nightmare was over. I do not know why this event sticks in my head. I just remember how young I was and never really having a belief in the Mormon religion. It was the complete opposite for Wanda. She lived for the Church, and she did what she could to prove that to other members of the church. Her life was absolutely consumed by Jesus and the Mormon faith, and her children were not going to get in the way of it. **I did not want a religion; I wanted a mother to love me more than anything or anyone.**

Going to Murray Park was another activity I enjoyed with my family. The park was not far from our house so we went there often. We usually went our separate ways at the park to do the activities we each enjoyed the most. There is a river that runs through the park, and Richard and I always went to fish on the river. My baby sister was about three at the time of this particular trip, and thanks to minimal supervision, she was already independent (she thought). While we fished the river, our sister Rachel approached us and asked if we had seen LouRee. We had not seen our little sister, so Rachel started to get scared.

"I've been looking all over for her," she nervously said.

Rachel asked for our help in finding her, and I said, "She's probably around somewhere."

Rachel left us and continued to search for LouRee. After a few minutes, I started to worry about LouRee so I dropped my fishing pole and went to help look for her. I found Rachel bent over giving LouRee a stern lecture, and I asked her what happened. Rachel informed me that in her search for LouRee, she chanced upon her in the parking lot walking with a strange man.

"LouRee where are you going?" Rachel asked LouRee firmly.

The man turned around, and when he saw Rachel standing there with a bead on him, he let go of LouRee's hand and quickly walked away. Rachel intercepted our baby sister from the stranger.

"That nice man was going to show me some puppies in his car." LouRee said innocently.

"LouRee, you can't ever do that again!" Rachel nervously warned her.

We told our mom what happened, and she called the police to report the attempted abduction. I do not think the man was ever apprehended, and I hope the sick bastard never got his hands on somebody else's child. LouRee was about twenty seconds away from being a kidnapped victim, and it scared us all. I would have never figured, at that time, my own mother would evolve into one of these Freaks.

Even though Ted beat up Wanda on a regular basis, I knew, in his own twisted way, he loved her. He would often cater to my mom's wishes, but it was financially difficult for him. Ted was in debt up to his eyeballs with the new organ and piano he bought for Wanda. The two musical instruments together must have cost more than twenty thousand dollars, but he bought them for her with very little complaining. My dad had to take on more jobs to support us, as well as our mom's expensive taste. Along with coaching and teaching Drivers-Ed, Ted began driving trucks at night to pay all of the expenses. It seemed whenever my mom wanted something, and Ted could not or would not get it for her, she would threaten a divorce, and he would cave in and buy it for her. He must have been doing *pretty well* in the income department because along with the organ and baby grand piano, Wanda talked our dad into buying a commercial oven to start a wedding cake business. Now, Wanda had everything she needed to keep herself very busy. This, of course, murdered the small amount of attention we received from her, and the jobs my dad held to pay for all of this started to wear on him. At this time our parents were constantly fighting, and I remember Wanda kicking my father out of the house for a few days at a time. When Ted was gone, Wanda would mope around the house until he called and manipulated his way back into her good graces. Once he was back, it would not take long for the abuse to start as before.

Violence now seemed to find me away from home, as well as at home. Other kids from around our neighborhood wanted a "piece of me". My siblings and I had to learn to stick-up for each other, and we certainly knew how to fight. One time when I was in the sixth grade, a tenth grader in the neighborhood wanted to kick my ass. I was terrified of him, so I told my sister Alicia.

"I'll take care of him for you Derrick," she told me, and she did.

After school, this kid twice my size waited for me to exit the bus. The good thing was, Alicia got off the bus before me and made the first move on him. He was standing half way to stupid when my sister tore into him. Alicia was not much bigger than I was, but she could fight. While she threw this giant, in my world around, she casually told him,

"You'd better not even think of touching Derrick." That bully could do nothing, but agree with her, and he never bothered me again. That boy walked home with a bloody nose, a torn shirt, and his tail between his legs. I thought it was cool that my sister did that for me, and I felt very grateful to her.

Somebody else moved into our neighborhood about a year later that didn't know better than to mess with me. I cannot remember exactly why he didn't like me, but it was probably over a girl. He was in the ninth grade, so he had two full grades on me. I was not really scared of this boy; I just did not want to fight him.

One weekend, he confronted me and said, "Monday, after school, I'm going to fight you whether you like it or not."

I did not like it, and all weekend wondered what I was going to do. Monday came, and on the bus ride home, he kept looking back at me while moving his lips.

"I'm going to kick your ass," was what I could clearly make out, and it boiled me over.

When the bus came to our stop, the dumb ass got up and started walking off the bus. I had to do something; I was just not sure what. He walked down the steps in front of me at the bus door, and that was when I saw my move. There was a small two-foot high fence at the bus stop. He walked off the last step and turned to face me. Before he turned all the way around, I ran down the stairs of the bus. I remember the look of shock on his face as I leaped off the last step, hitting him with the full force of my ten-year old body. My momentum flipped him over the fence, and he tore his pants on a nail that stuck out of it. I found myself on top of him with my little fists working his face like a side of beef, and I felt like Rocky. Soon, I noticed a large crowd cheering me on. I stopped tenderizing his face and realized what was going on. I immediately started crying and plead to the crowd, "I don't want to fight him." I then turned back to him and repeated the same thing to him as I pulled myself from his chest. Of course, everybody was calling me a "pussy", and I must have looked stupid for crying after throttling this kid, but I saw my father's rage in me, and it scared me. I realized at a young age that I did not want to be like my father, but my ignorance did not allow me to be unlike him, at that time. **By ten years old, I knew I was not a violent person, but that was about it.**

From fighting, and starting fires, I evolved into a thief. A friend in my neighborhood showed me his dad's rifle. The gun was kept in their garage. I had grown bored with my BB gun so with the rifle in my sights, I wanted the bigger gun. After a little planning, the gun was in my hands, and I headed to the field by my house to hide it. I removed the scope from the weapon and buried the scope in the dirt. I put the gun back in the case, hid it under some brush, and went home. At ten years old, I did not make a good criminal. I started bragging at the bus stop about a .22 I had found out in the field, and soon the kid I took the gun from approached me.

"We're missing a .22," he said.

"Oh this one can't be yours; it doesn't have a scope," I said nervously.

That evening, my mother woke me from my sleep.

"Derrick there are some Detectives here that want to talk to you," she said.

I went to the kitchen table and joined the two Detectives. My heart felt like it was going to pop out of my chest while they questioned me.

"We heard you found a gun, Derrick," one of the officers said.

"Yeah I did," I cautiously told them.

"Can you tell us how you found it and where it is?" he asked.

I immediately fabricated a story about two guys that I saw running through the field while I was lizard hunting. I said something to the fact that they were holding a firearm case, and I saw them drop it.

"Can you describe them for us?" one of them asked.

"Older, white kids wearing Hawaiian shirts," I choked.

I must have been watching too much Hawaii 5-0 at the time, because it was all I could come up with. I don't know how they kept a straight face and managed not to laugh at me right there. They came back the next day and had me show them where the rifle was, and they also got me to confess to the crime. I was not stupid enough to drag that lie out any farther.

I was absolutely fascinated with firearms, and I was not learning anything about stealing. The only thing I knew was, if caught, I would just get an ass kicking, and I survived many of those, so fear was not a factor now. One time I was at a young girlfriend's house. I found her father's .22 caliber pistol. I figured it was more inconspicuous than the rifle I had stolen earlier because of its small size so I took it home and hid it in my closet. I loved the weapon, and remember staring at the barrel while the bullets filled the chamber. I was fascinated by the mechanics and the look of the pistol. I thought it would be cool to take it to school and show my friends. The pistol made the journey with me into my seventh grade class. I kept it in the front of my pants. My Teacher was having a discussion with us on a subject I do not recall, when I decided to show the weapon.

"Hey Steve, check this out," I said to the student in front of me. He turned around and gazed at the pistol's handle sticking out of my pants.

"That's cool," he said.

As he turned farther around to stare at the weapon, our Teacher bellowed, "What is that?"

My heart sank to my ass. I looked up and thought for sure he was talking to me. Steve turned back around, and I lowered my shirt over the pistol.

"What is that?" the Teacher asked again. A female student that was sitting right behind me finally replied, "It's a note."

"Throw it away," he said.

She stood up, walked to the trash and threw the note away. Thinking I was busted for sure, I decided school was not the best place to take a gun. I managed to get the weapon home without killing anyone, but it did not stay there long. My girlfriend's dad figured out that I took it and demanded its safe return or he would call the police. I really did not want any more trouble with the law over firearms so I returned the pistol and no longer had a girlfriend. Ted was tired of me stealing weapons, and his appearance to outsiders was a priority for him, I guess he decided if he bought me a gun, I would not steal anymore, and a short time later, I had my own 410 Shotgun. My bad behavior seemed corrected, although I didn't learn anything by it.

Our dysfunctional family made it to a family reunion in Colorado one year. After the usual activities of the reunion, it got boring so we decided to do something fun for ourselves. Wanda stayed back at camp, and the rest of the family went for a ride to find a hill to hike. We found a nice looking hill that appeared we could all easily climb. Before the hike, Ted lectured us on rattlesnakes and what to do if we spotted one.

"Don't run, stand still, and let them get out of the way;" I clearly remember him saying. "They're more afraid of you than you are of them;" I recall him saying, also.

I have always loved reptiles so I was looking forward to seeing a snake, if I could. The hike started with LouRee, in front, on my dad's shoulders, and me in the rear of our family chain as we paraded up the hill. I wanted to be at the back of the line so I could turn over rocks in hopes of finding a snake. I was nearing the top of the hill when I heard my father yell, "Snake!" Ted was at the top of the hill, and he set LouRee down and ran, passing his children in the opposite direction. Soon, they were all running down the hill opposite of me. I continued up the hill because I had to see that snake. I made it as far as my baby sister who was still near the snake. LouRee was only four at the time and did not know a rattlesnake from a squeaky toy. According to my father, it was a large rattlesnake heading up the hill trying to avoid any contact with us (so, my dad was right about that part). My sister was consumed by fear and frozen in her tracks. I felt something I had never experienced before in my life. When I came upon LouRee and saw how terrified she was, I knew I had to help her. My whole hike, to this point, consisted of my determination to see a snake, but when I saw my sister completely frozen with fear, I felt a sense of responsibility, and I knew what I had to do. There was a small 4-foot dirt shelf separating us. I coached her to slide down the hill on her bottom; which she did, and she landed in my arms. I set her down and grabbed her hand, and we walked to our family below. I recall being very upset with my father. I could not comprehend why he would leave LouRee there like that. We made our way back to the reunion where I told everyone about Ted being a chicken shit, and, as you may imagine, we teased him about that for several years, but he did nothing about it. He was busted and branded a coward as far as I was concerned.

CHAPTER THREE:
TOO PREY

With all the offensive behavior that I, and other members of my family, unloaded on the neighborhood, our reputation in Sandy turned sour. Members of our church ward became annoyed with the drama that was oozing from our doors. Ted and Wanda were not doing well, and the bills from Wanda's Holy Musical Instruments (HMIs) made life even harder on us all. With our family in complete disarray, and the bills far exceeding my father's income, it was time to get out of Sandy.

My dad found us a house in West Valley, Utah, and Wanda's baby grand piano and commercial oven were sold. A Century 21 sign was put in the front yard, and shortly after, our home was passed over to another big Mormon family. We said goodbye to our friends, loaded our memories in mind and left. I loved our house in Sandy, and I recall feeling very sad when it sold. After eight years in our faux heaven, we were moving farther from heaven and closer to hell. Instability was a cornerstone in our family, and at eleven years old, I had three moves under my juvenile belt. Along with several friends that came and went, I never really got accustomed to any of my schools.

I finally established myself in the eighth grade at Valley Junior High. I was a "Liger" because of the school mascot's strange background. The story, from what I know, is that a cub born at our local Zoo was of mixed parents, one a lion and the other a tiger; hence the appropriate title, "Liger."

In the first days at my new school, I found myself in a lot of trouble due to several students not liking me. I heard some talk of a kid named Greg who was going to kick my ass to China in our gym locker room. I don't think I was in school a week when he wanted to fight me. While I was in the Gym locker room getting dressed, Greg and his friends came in to see "what I was made of". I never cared much for fighting because I hated what I turned into when I got angry. I made a dramatic speech about how I would rather be Greg's friend than his enemy, and he backed down. We shook hands and became best friends, almost immediately.

I enjoyed being in the eighth grade. I was making friends, and I was able to avoid our house while I was either in school, or over at one of my new friend's houses. Greg lived a short walk from me, and we did almost everything together.

Greg's house was separated from a busy side street by an old cedar fence. This house had a prime location for me to plot an idea to give us some cheap entertainment. With a box of old clothes Greg's mother allocated for Church charity and some old newspapers, we fabricated our dummies. We waited until dark then carried the stuffed bodies onto the road when the coast was clear. We ran back into Greg's yard and peeked through knotholes in the fence as the cars approached our paper filled people. Some of the drivers slowed down, and drove around the dummies. Other people slammed on their brakes, coming to a stop, just inches from them.

"Holy shit; is he alright," I heard someone say.

"Somebody's just playing around," a man said. The man grabbed the dummy, put it in his trunk and drove away.

We went through a couple of dummies that night until it got boring for us, and we moved on to something else. Greg and I shared two common interests; one was firearms and the other fireworks. We did the normal boy things like pouring gasoline on our plastic models and setting them ablaze. Attaching multiple firecrackers to various objects and blowing them to bits. Also making miniature cannons from spent rifle casings and having small-scale wars with them. Greg still lacked one thing I was looking for, somebody to party with.

I made a friend at school named Preston who was a little more rowdy than Greg. Preston lived with his single mom and little sister. I thought Preston was cool because he was popular with the girls. He always had one or more girls talking to him at any given time, and the fact that Preston wanted to hang out with me, made me feel just as hip as he was. I knew I really was not, but I wanted to be. Preston introduced me to a girl who I took a fancy to, and some days we walked home together. Her name was Karen, and she lived only a couple of blocks from our school. Karen's house was on the street I walked home on so it was easy for me to meet her after school and talk to her as I walked her the short way home.

I missed her leaving school one day, so I hurried up the street to try and intercept her. I arrived at her house as she was coming out her front door, and I noticed she did not look very happy.

"You should smile more," I said with my smoothest charm.

She looked at me for a brief moment. She did not say anything, but quickly went to her neighbor's house. She looked distressed so I left her alone, but I wondered what was troubling her. The next day at school, I learned that about a minute before I walked by Karen's house the previous day. She entered her house and discovered her mother and her only sister dead in her home. While Karen was in school that day, her mom's boyfriend took a gun and executed everyone in the house, and then he turned the gun on himself. I had no idea this had happened when I walked by her house and tried to talk to her, nonetheless, I still felt uncomfortable about the whole situation.

Karen came back to school about a week later, and I apologized to her for the loss of her family. She said "thanks", but due to the tragedy we ended up going our separate ways. Karen left our school a short time later, and I never heard from her again. **I felt like I was always surrounded by tragedy, and I did not know how to handle it.**

Preston showed up to school one day with a short Mohawk that ran up the back of his head. After about an inch rise, the Mohawk parted, perfectly, down the middle of his head and ended in a curl. The girls at school could not leave it alone, and his popularity level rose even more. I immediately figured I needed a Mohawk, and I talked Preston into cutting my hair. My Mohawk was not as cool as his because of our different hair types so the girls did not give me the same attention Preston received.

Preston invited me to his house to drink beer with him. I did not ask many questions. I just went over to drink with him so he wouldn't have to drink alone. I did, on one occasion, inquire where he was getting the beer at his young age of 14. He swore me to secrecy and told me one of his teachers was getting it for him. I felt very uncomfortable the one time I saw his teacher sitting on Preston's couch. Looking back, the guy had to be some kind of a creep to supply young teen boys with alcohol. Preston and I were good friends, but Greg and I did everything together.

On Greg's 13th birthday, he and I along with Richard went to a local ski resort to do some night skiing. I was not skiing long before I went down a hill and spotted a jump that ran off the trail, and it called my name. I answered the call and went off the jump. I did not make it all the way over, but instead fell off the edge. As I fell, my ski came off and ran across my head; cutting a deep wound in the top of my skull. The injury was quite severe, but Greg and Richard did not want to leave yet so they continued skiing. I found myself in a familiar position. I was badly injured at a ski resort waiting for medical attention. This time it was not as bad as my ski injury when I was younger because the Ski Patrol wrapped my head in bandages and bought me a couple of beers to drink while I waited for my ride. By the time Ted came and picked us up, my blood had soaked through the bandages, and I was in a lot of pain. He took me to the emergency room, and I received about a dozen stitches in my head.

I had the stitches in for a few weeks until they started to make my head itch. My parents were so neglectful that it was several days past time to have them removed. I told Preston about my predicament, and he said he could remove them. I went over to his house, and he sat me down in the bathroom so he could get a good look at his upcoming task. After a quick look, he retrieved some tweezers and a small pair of scissors to cut the sutures. At first, he grabbed the wrong end of the stitches and pulled the stitches tighter in my head. I screamed in pain, and soon Preston realized he grabbed the wrong end. After he realized his mistake, he grabbed the right end, and I felt the stitches unravel from my head. I thanked my friend and went home. I thought my parents would be proud of me since they didn't have to take me back to the doctor for the removal of my stitches, but they were not. I thought Preston did them a favor by saving them some time and money, but instead they lectured me on infections, and how I should not do that again.

"Well maybe if some people did their job as a parent in the first place, I would not have to ask my friend for a medical favor," I thought as Ted bitched me out.

All Ted and Wanda talked about at this time of my life was how we no longer had any money. I remember wanting to wear Levi 501 jeans, but with six children in the house, they were always too expensive to buy. I felt like the only kid in school, besides my brother Richard, wearing Toughskins. It seemed all of my peers at school had *something* to say about my stupid jeans. Our move to the cheaper home in West Valley did not help my school fashion, and I was soon to find out how poor we were now. Thanks to my father's generous donations to the church over the years, they accepted us into their Welfare Program. Now, the church provided us with clothes and food. However, the food was nasty, and the clothes looked even worse than the Toughskins I complained about. Sometimes my friend, Greg would come over and see the Deseret milk in our refrigerator and tease us. We had to stir the peanut butter because of the thick layer of oil that covered it, and the chili had big chunks of beef vein throughout, so I had to pick them out before I could eat it. I knew it was Church welfare, and it was not suppose to be the highest quality or best tasting stuff, and I was hungry so I accepted it with little complaining.

Wanda did not like the food or clothes from the church so she still bought the things she wanted. It was typical to see my mother come home and run through the house with a bag of McDonalds. She would hurry to her room and lock the door before any of her children could ask for some. The intoxicating smell of french-fries overpowered our peanut butter & oil sandwich, but she wouldn't offer us any. Wanda became more and more selfish, and Ted was scarce from working so much. "Come on people you've got children over here!" I complained to myself.

Ted continued driving trucks part-time when we moved to West Valley, and sometimes he came to our house at night to take one of his children with him. He drove for Milne Truck Lines, and most of the time he pulled triples (three trailers). Our home was nestled in a tight neighborhood, and I loved it when he pulled up to get one of us. I would look out the window and see the big truck blocking driveways three houses down. I knew one of us was going for a ride. The rides were not long, about 25 miles, but I thought it was great being in a "big rig" with my dad. Driving the truck out of the neighborhood was quite tricky, but Ted managed it well. I remember him swinging the "semi" in large half- circles, and driving on people's lawns and sidewalks to maneuver the trailers out of the neighborhood. I loved these times with my father because it was the only time I could let my guard down, and be myself without fear of repercussion from him. Sometimes Ted tried to be a good dad, but my father was crippled when it came to showing genuine love. **It seemed all I knew how to do; was act out and receive negative attention, but I wanted to be loved.**

A collection of guns found their way into my room. Some were from my father, and some I made at school. I had a basement room with a built-in dresser in the wall. After I pulled out a few drawers, I had an indoor shooting range. I lined up bottles along the back of the wall and fired at them with a .45 caliber muzzle-loader that I made in school, I doubt they allow kids to make those in shop classes anymore, but that was what I did.

I had a collection of airplane models, and four of them were hanging from my ceiling. While Greg was over one day, I decided to shoot the planes out of the sky with my rifle.

"Hey Greg watch this" I said, and then I blew the airplanes out of the sky while Greg stood shocked and amazed. The sound of gunfire rang through the house, but no one ever said anything about it. The only ones at home that day; were my siblings, Greg, and me. I think everybody was afraid to come downstairs and see what I was shooting at.

At the age of thirteen I had started smoking pot. One day, a friendly neighborhood pot deal went bad, and the kid I was buying the *weed* from punched me in the nose. I ran home to extract my revenge by shooting him with my .22 caliber rifle. Two of my older siblings were home, and they pinned me down on my bed to prevent me from leaving the house with my gun. My detainment did not stop me from firing the weapon, and the bullet passed through the bathroom and into the storage room where it exploded a can of tomato sauce. Luckily, nobody was sitting on the toilet in the bathroom at that time. After seeing the shocking aftermath of the bullet wound to the tomato sauce can, I understood shooting someone was not a smart idea.

Shooting holes in everything was typical of me, back then. Through my church, I became a Boy Scout, and I thought my Scout Leaders were so cool. One of them was missing some fingers from playing with dynamite blasting caps. "Sweet!" I thought.

Most of our scouting trips consisted of us going into a sagebrush field and shooting everything that moved. Rabbit hunting became an activity we did almost every weekend, and they taught us to do it well. There were ten Boy Scouts, me being one of them, and we would form a line and walked through the brush, systematically, eliminating hundreds of rabbits. We were not taught to care about any of these lives we took, and we started doing disrespectful things to the dead animals. We were carelessly pissing on dead bunnies and shooting pregnant mommy rabbits. We thought we were tough, "Go Scouts".

Richard was given a Ruger 10/22 from Ted, and it was fully equipped to wipe out several rabbits at a time. He had two 50-round clips, and it was fun to see how fast we could empty them. While walking in our usual death line, a rabbit escaped through our wall of lead, and it ran in between us. Richard's semi-automatic weapon followed the rabbit and bullets flew all around us. Fortunately, nobody was hurt, and Richard felt pretty bad about swinging his weapon behind us.

Our Scout Leaders also knew how to make and use explosives. They did this kind of work at their day jobs, and they passed the knowledge on to us. I was taught many things about explosives. From making bottle rockets out of model rocket engines, to the basic fabrication of pipe bombs. There wasn't a pipe bomb merit badge, but if there were, I certainly would have earned one.

"Shoot the container," one of our Scout leaders said to my friend.

My friend shot and missed a Prestone, Anti-Freeze bottle that sat on a hill, about a hundred yards away. Our Scout Master reloaded the gun and took aim at the container. "Bang!" the weapon went off, and when the bullet met with the plastic bottle, it instantly exploded. A large "BOOM!!" echoed through the canyon, and a big crater was left behind. We tried to get him to tell us what was in the bottle, but he would not say. Probably not a good idea to tell us anyway, I suppose. These are just a few things we learned in the Boy Scouts.

When I did things for the Church, it was not because I wanted to, but because my friends did them, along with some really hot Mormon chicks. At thirteen, I baptized for the dead. Yep, you heard right. Baptizing for the dead is strictly a Mormon thing, I think. I guess this is why there are so many temples; it's where the Mormons perform their Holy work for "God Almighty" himself.

Several children from our local ward, including me, were crammed into a van and driven to the Salt Lake Temple. This was a weird experience for me. Strange people herded us into a room to change our clothes and put on plain, white jumpsuits. Then they walked us, in a line, to a large baptismal fount that stood on the backs of some big, white cow statues. We had to walk up several stairs to get in the water. There was a man standing in front of us, holding a list of names. Another man stood next to the first teenager in line. While the man with the list read off the name of somebody that had been dead for a while, the other man would dunk the boy in the water. This was repeated over and over.

In the name of Derrick Thompson: I baptize you

(insert dead person's name here), to the true church of Christ.

The speech was something along those lines and I recall it *freaking* me out.

They kept us in a circle in the water, and after one person was dunked, the next one in line would get it. This went on for several minutes until the list of names was read. Since I didn't believe in any of this, every dead person that was baptized in my name probably dodged a spiritual bullet and did not become a member of the Mormon faith. I thought it was very arrogant of the Church to baptize dead people. I wondered if they had permission from the families of the deceased or if they were so vain, they just took it upon themselves.

My dad was arrogant, as well as ignorant, and he made many comments about other religions. He typically spoke badly about Catholics.

"Catholics are devil worshipers," he would say.

His ignorance bothered me so I questioned his comments. "What makes you believe Catholics are devil worshipers?" I asked smartly.

"Because, if you ever read their teachings, you'll just know," he replied with the knowledge of a two-year old.

When my dad practiced religious prejudice, it made me pull away from the Mormon faith even more. Ted spoke highly of his church and poorly of people who were not members. He could act any way he wanted, but he just knew he would still be saved during the "second coming of Christ" - because he's Mormon.

Sex was on my mind, as well as everyone else's around me, it seemed. Experimenting with sex, in one way or another, appeared to be the norm. I acquired some Playboys from a friend of mine, and I put them to good use when I wanted to relieve my sexual desire. I did my best impersonation of a "zoo monkey" pleasuring himself. At this same stage of my life, my bishop from church wanted to talk to me. I cannot remember why Mormon bishops have these meetings with Mormon children at adolescent age, but it is uniform.

"Do you pay your tithing?" He asked me casually.

"Not really," I replied.

"Paying your tithing will bring blessings in your life," he said.

"Yeah, you're a fucking idiot!" I thought, but said, "So, they tell me."

I had the opportunity of watching my father write several-hundred dollar checks per month to the Church, and if it blessed us, I had yet to see those blessings.

Then he asked the question that floored me, "Do you masturbate?"

I didn't know what to say. "Are you supposed to be asking me that?" I wondered. After a short pause, I gave a resounding "No."

It was a very embarrassing question, and it freaked me out. The conversation didn't go on for much longer. After our meeting, I went home, shaking my head. The Bishop must have assumed I was lying because, a couple of days later, my father found the porno magazines under my bed.

"These aren't good to have," he told me and took them away. I would bet money he looked at them.

Here I was, a hormonal teen with my magazines stolen from me, and my young eyes feeling the need to gaze upon breasts. Without my nudie magazines, I felt the need to take my sexuality out of the privacy of my bedroom. Richard and I befriended some neighborhood girls. Their parents owned a Chinese restaurant and were hardly ever home. We would go over to their house, watch porno movies, and play strip poker. "Stroking her budding clitoris" and, "Now, it's time to mount her." were part of my vocabulary as a young teen, thanks to porno movies, but the girls would not give us any *real* action, so it was time to try elsewhere.

A friend of Richard's that lived a few houses away from us had a girlfriend whom was already having sex at twelve years old. They were pre-teen swingers. We had a plan to take a turn having sex with this girl. One evening we went to her house while her parents were gone. Richard's friend went first because it was his girlfriend. Richard went second, and when it was my turn, I went into her living room and saw her lying on the floor. I was more than ready, but for some reason I could not penetrate her. After a few times trying to enter her, I gave up and finished-off in her bedroom. Besides the incest, this was the first time I tried to have sex. I thought I knew what to do, but that was not the case. These activities were tame compared to what was happening to our brother, Brad. Richard and I were still involved on some level, but our older brother was in the deepest.

A truck pulled up to our house at about 11:00 pm. It was my brother, Brad and a neighborhood friend of his, David. They invited my younger brother and me to go downtown with them and find a hooker. Being young boys, we thought this would be fun so we jumped in the truck, and went downtown. After driving around for a short time, we spotted an African American woman dressed in skimpy clothing, and we decided she was the one we wanted.

David pulled the truck up next to her and asked "How much?"

She seemed stunned by a truck full of boys, and she asked us if we were joking. The older boys quickly responded, "No," which left her to respond, "How much you got?"

"Five bucks," my older brother said proudly.

She gave us a look of complete confusion, and replied with, "Oh, you guys are just playing." With that, she turned and walked away, and we drove home.

I do recall thinking, "They took us all the way downtown to find a hooker with only five dollars?" Even I knew, you needed more than that, especially for one adult and three teens. This was one of my first experiences with Brad's friend, David. He lived across the street from us.

David came over to our house one day, and he asked Richard and me if we wanted to be in a book he was writing. We had no idea what he was writing about, but we figured it would be fun to be in his book. We walked across the street to his house, and we went in his downstairs room where he asked us some very personal questions. He began wanting to know minor details about us, and then he got real personal. David offered us a plethora of porno magazines, and we were looking at them while he was asking us his questions.

"How big would you say your penis is?" He asked me, and I responded while David jotted notes down.

"Six inches," I proudly said.

"Are you serious?" David asked. "Usually that's the average size for an adult male," he replied.

I reassured him my figures were correct, and then he asked if he could see it. I felt the question was quite odd, but being a young teen I complied with the request and whipped it out. Richard exposed his penis as well. When David saw our peckers pointing skyward, he pulled his out and began masturbating. This made my younger brother and me very uncomfortable, so we zipped-up and zipped-out of there.

After this incident, Richard and I stopped hanging around David. I later found out that my older brother was sexually involved with David, and our next-door neighbor, Kim took a shine towards Brad also.

I met Kim shortly after we moved into our home. She seemed nice enough, and she was a good Mormon housewife, or so she had people believe. I don't remember what her husband did for a living, but he looked like he could have been a Lumber Jack. Whatever he did, he was hardly ever home. Kim was our friend. She helped us out with certain things because of our money situation. When our mom expressed a concern about how she was going to pay for school clothes one year, Kim stepped-up and offered to buy them for us. Ocean Pacific was the popular brand at the time, and Kim bought me 200 dollars worth of the clothes.

Everything appeared to be great with the relationship our family had with Kim, and we spent plenty of time at her house. Brad was spending the most time over there. Kim had a son Brad's age, and Brad and he shared common interests. I assumed that was why my brother went to their house so often. Then, one day when Brad and I were at Kim's house, I suddenly found myself alone. After a short while, I walked upstairs and saw Brad walking out of Kim's bedroom. Kim came out a short time later. It was very odd to me, so I confronted Brad about it.

"What were you guys doing?" I asked him.

He did not give up the information while we were still at Kim's house, but later at home he told me they were having sex. I was envious of my older brother, and I remember wanting to have sex with Kim also. She was an average-looking woman, but I was not after looks. I was an unguided teenager with a gigantic sex drive. I made a few attempts to woo her, with no success. I guess she wanted somebody seventeen not thirteen, at least she had *some* morals (that was sarcasm).

When my oldest sister, Rachel reached dating age, She began to date David. He was her age. My sister was oblivious to how David was when she was not around. David and Brad were experimenting with homosexuality behind her back. Yes, Brad was having sex with David and Kim during the same time frame. He was caught in a "powder-keg" of a love triangle, and it was soon to explode.

David and Rachel obtusely became engaged, but that was not going to last long. From what I recall, Rachel found out about David and Brad having sex, and she put an end to her engagement, as well as her relationship with David. David did not accept the break-up so he developed a plan with Brad to win Rachel back. This plan ended up changing their lives. The two were downstairs, in a storage room at David's house, and Brad placed a rifle on the back of David's upper-right arm, and pulled the trigger. The bullet punched through his bone and exited through the front of his bicep. An ambulance arrived at David's house soon after the shooting, and the paramedics took him out on a stretcher. Our neighborhood was in complete chaos due to this sick plot.

David was trying to gain sympathy from my sister with the bullet wound to his arm, and my brother was trying to escape his life - through the doors of an adolescent mental ward. The plan did not work in David's favor, but my older brother was whisked away to the LDS Hospital Psychiatric Ward. Thus, my older brother was where he needed to be, and I felt envious of him because he was out of our "messed-up" home. This is my recollection of the events, but as I learned later, this story goes even deeper into dysfunction.

My father was in the Air National Guard, and he was called to duty in Germany for three months. Brad was a computer genius at an early age, and one of our neighbors gave him an old computer. Brad created games on the computer, and he, Richard, and I spent a lot of time playing those games. One evening, the three of us were downstairs playing a game in Brad's room, and Wanda appeared at the bedroom door. She was distraught, and she was holding a kitchen knife to her wrist.

"I'm going to kill myself tonight. Brad you have to help me," our sick mother said.

As she spoke, tears rolled down her face. I could see her hand applying more pressure to her wrist with the knife.

Richard and I could not believe what we were witnessing right before our eyes. Brad stood up, as if this were an every day event, and casually walked out the door with her. I didn't know what was going on at that moment. It was just dreadfully weird to me and it made me uncomfortable to be around my mom.

My sister, LouRee told me later in life that my mother was having sex with my older brother. With our father gone, my older brother was the man of the house, and his duties included sex with our mom, I guess. When LouRee was seven, she walked in on my mother, Kim, and Brad engaged in a twisted threesome on more than one occasion. During our discussions several years later, LouRee and I concluded this was probably the major reason Brad shot David. It was a traumatic way to get out of our house, but it worked.

Wanda's sick and perverted mind was in bloom, and it was only going to get worse. I heard from some of Wanda's family members, she was molested as a child by one of her music Teachers. It was not even on the same level with the kind of things Wanda did with her oldest son and the neighbor lady, and as I find myself reflecting on it, I am confused at its origin.

With my father away in Germany, we rowdy children became more wild and uncontrollable. Wanda did not have the physical control over us that our father had, and truthfully, just didn't care about us. My mother started turning to the Bishop from our ward for advice, and from what I understood, it was not good for our family or for Ted. I do not know if the years of physical abuse finally wore on her or what, but I believe the

Bishop was preparing Wanda to leave my father. I wondered if she told the Bishop she was having sex with her son?

With our dad gone, Wanda was free to get rid of her children, as well. One night she snapped on us, and kicked her kids out of the house. She gave us enough time to pack a few clothes, and then she booted us out, not really caring where we went. Most of us were scattered around the neighborhood at various friends' houses. If I recall correctly, my younger siblings and I spent a few days with friends, and our older siblings found shelter elsewhere. I did not know where, but we were not gone long because our father was soon to be home from Germany. With Wanda fearing Ted's wrath, she let us back in the house after a short vacation from us.

CHAPTER FOUR:
THE ALPHA MALE

The stress my mother caused to herself started taking its toll on her. Wanda's poor mental health condition worsened. My father was stressed also, and he liked to use that as an excuse to thrash us. In between our beatings, I would argue with him. Most of my arguments with him now were about how I hated Church and did not want to go anymore. My younger brother and I did everything we could to avoid church. After sacrament meeting, we were gone from our parent's site. We would "sluff" Sunday school and hide under the stage in the gymnasium. We were to a point where it was more fun to sit in complete darkness, than it was to go to Church.

At the age of thirteen, Mormon boys are given the responsibility to break the bread for sacrament meeting. I had already been doing this for a little while, and when Richard turned thirteen, he started helping. We didn't team up long before we screwed up this Church duty. Being the poor, starving, kid/hellions we were; Richard and I took the whole loaf of bread we were supposed to break into pieces for sacrament, we wadded it up in two giant bread balls, and we ate them. Someone from the church had to go to the store and buy another loaf of bread. We were pretty proud when we made that Mormon shop on Sunday because it's against the religion to do so. We were not allowed to do that job anymore.

Finally, when I was fourteen years old, my father said, "You don't have to go to Church anymore."

"Well, thank you dad" I said to him. That was some of the best news I had heard in my life. Richard and I declined to attend church with our family from then on. Ted finally came to the realization that I was never going to believe in the Mormon religion, so he finally gave up trying.

Ted and Wanda's 20-year rollercoaster relationship was coming to a close now. **Wanda figured if she could not kick us out, she would just have to leave, and Ted let her go this time**. I remember my father being very depressed, but it seemed there was nothing he could do to make her stay.

We were barely in West Valley for a couple of years, and our individual lives were starting to take shape. Around the time of my parents' separation, Rachel was involved with another guy, and they were in love. If memory serves me correctly, Brad found an apartment with his girlfriend, and he moved away at this time as well. My sister, Alicia found comfort in a foster home so she was gone. Wanda was having a nervous breakdown at the time of the separation and went to live with a sister, I think. It all happened very fast, and we were traumatized by it. My clear thoughts are of me worrying about my two younger siblings and myself, and what was going to happen to us.

After a short separation, Wanda filed for a divorce, and this destroyed our father. Our house was put up for sale and Ted found a job at the Tooele Army Depot, as a security guard. He picked up the few tattered remains of his family and moved himself and his three youngest children to the Army Depot. I did not hear much about my mother for the next several months. Wanda went into hiding; from what I understood, and for the first time of my life, she was physically gone. I consoled my dad on a couple occasions, and I tried to put a positive spin on what happened to him.

"She was ugly anyway dad," I told him. "She wasn't a good mom either," I continued.

Ted shrugged it off, but I knew he was a hollow shell inside. It was a good feeling for me to say that to him. I was not fifteen yet, but I knew, all too well, the true nature of my mother.

Our big family was chopped in half, and so was our father. He was completely depressed with his situation, but with our mother wanting nothing to do with him or us, he attempted to step up. My father's parenting skills were next to none, which left his remaining children to continue fending for themselves.

Once settled in at our new home on post of the Tooele Army Depot. With the Depot a few miles from town, we felt isolated from the rest of the world. We lived in a small community of social rejects, so we fit right in.

Our mother wanted nothing to do with us. She never called or visited. Ted took us to her house a few times, but she hardly said anything to her children. My parents would try to carry on civil conversations with one another, but it usually turned into an argument, and we would leave. It seemed we never went over to my mom's house just to visit, it was always so they could fight, and I hated it.

Wanda was suffering from a complete mental collapse and our dad, in no way, cared what we did. This was having a profound affect on me. **I cared less and less for my mother, and I also cared less about myself or about the consequences of my actions**. At this point, I had already been through a river of shit, and I was not yet ready to go ashore. I figure; with my parents being the pathetic guardians they were, I had to learn everything through trial and error. The trials were usually long and the errors were frequent.

We three youngest children found ourselves in a familiar situation. We lived in a home on a dead-end circle, isolated from other people by miles of road and sagebrush. With no parental guidance to speak of, we had nowhere to go but down, and looking back, the trip was fast. There were three main places for people in this small community to go. One was a bar, one a recreation center, and the last was a small bowling alley with an arcade in it.

Richard and I made a friend that lived with his alcoholic grandmother. If she was not working, she was passed out from alcohol. While she was at work, we had the perfect opportunity to steal her booze, and we did. When we three young teens were drunk on alcohol there was sure to be trouble for us.

Sometimes me, Richard, and our new friend went to the bar; they would not sell us alcohol, but we thought it was hip to order virgin Shirley Temples and pretend we were grown-up like the rest of the people there. Sometimes we would visit the recreation center and try our hand at racket ball or weight lifting, but the bowling alley had an arcade, so most of our time was allocated to it. This is not where our life of crime started, but we were definitely honing our skills as junior criminals here. The arcade was in a room separate from the bowling lanes, and there was usually only one person behind the counter passing out shoes. One day, we noticed that the backs of the video-game machines were not secured, and with the proper plan, their money could be ours. Our friend kept a lookout, my brother pretended to play the machine, and I squeezed behind it and took the back off. JACKPOT! Inside the video game, someone had placed a big plywood box to hold the influx of quarters, and the box was loaded. With a little backward-force, the box ripped from its base, and we filled our pockets with quarters. We did this with a couple machines a day until we exhausted them.

With our pockets filled with quarters, we would run outside the bowling alley and count our loot. There are a large number of stupid criminals out there, and we were certainly no exception. Being misguided and malnourished children, we would go back inside the bowling alley after calculating our funds to buy food and candy with the quarters. Needless to say, it did not take long for the bowling alley employees to catch on to our little scheme, and we were busted.

One day Ted came home and asked us why FBI agents wanted to talk to us about stolen money. We played stupid for a short while, but eventually the FBI sat us down, and got us to confess about breaking into the video games. Our father had to pay for whatever money was missing so, luckily, we told them we only took about three dollars in change. They, of course, knew it was more than that, but they had no way of knowing how much money was actually there (about 100 times that). Ted wrote out a check for three dollars, and we could no longer go to the bowling alley. We escaped that incident with no severe beatings from our father, and a somewhat untouchable feeling because we fooled some G-Men. Our friend's grandmother would not let him hang out with us anymore, so we had to find other things to do.

Our sister Rachel and her fiancé, Steve came to visit us sometimes, and our activities with them included getting high or drinking. I thought Rachel's future husband was one of the greatest guys I knew. The local Tooele Mountains became one of our favorite places to hang out, so when they came over, they usually took us there. Rachel and Steve were not trying to be our parents; they just wanted to spend time with us. Richard and I did not mind at all.

Steve had an old Dodge Charger that he would take us to the mountains in. We would find a place to park, and then we would party until the early morning hours. Going back down the mountain in the dark was always intense. Steve would turn out the head lights and say, "Incognito."

"Okay Steve that's enough, turn the lights back on" Rachel would tell him.

I knew what we were doing was not safe or smart, but what can I tell you, except, that I was with an older sibling, and it was great to have her companionship. Richard and I loved the attention Rachel and Steve gave us, so we cherished our times with them. I thought about my other siblings often, and sometimes I wondered what my mother was doing. I felt she did not care for me so why should I care for her? My resentment for my mom continued to grow.

I never cared for the way my dad treated me or other members of our family, but he was my only parent so sometimes, I made half-assed attempts to do well for him. At Tooele High, I joined the football team and easily made the starting squad. My dad showed up to my football games, and I enjoyed seeing him there. When Ted came to my games, I really turned up my playing level and usually did very well. At one game, I made three interceptions and my dad could not have been happier. After that game, I heard something from my dad I had not before, encouragement.

"Derrick you played very well," he told me. "I think you could get a scholarship to play football, if you keep it up," he finished.

"I'm too short to play college ball," I reminded him.

"Nonsense. I played for BYU, and you're taller than me," he fired back.

I knew my destiny was not to play football, but it was still nice to hear the kudos. I took the pep talk my dad gave me and put it away. I soon discovered something else I liked better than football. The east parking lot at my High School; it was where all the stoners would hang out, and I wanted to be around the stoners more than the jocks. **Soon, I was no longer playing football. Instead, I was sluffing classes and getting high.**

As I entered my English class one day, somebody noticed the powerful aroma of marijuana smoke on me, and I received the nickname, "Joint." I got a kick out of it and began hanging out with people who had similar names, like "Burnout."

Skipping classes became a regular thing for me, and before the end of my tenth grade year, I dropped out of school. Ted either did not have the mental resources to cope with my reckless behavior, or he was just fed up, so he stopped caring what Richard and I did altogether. He was on to Richard's and my drinking and sluffing, but the way he handled it was to say, "Make sure you do it at a friend's house, so you don't drink and drive." Ted also caught me chewing tobacco, and he told me, "I'd rather see you smoking than chewing tobacco." I, then, started smoking cigarettes. The only things I learned from my father seemed to be the wrong things, and whatever I taught myself was most likely going to be wrong also.

My collection of guns was now bigger than ever, and I knew almost everything about them. I was able to completely take them apart to clean them. Also, disassemble the bullets and shotgun shells to experiment with my own homemade ammo. I would take the lead pellets from the shotgun shells and pull the bullets off my 22 shells. Using them in combination, I could make small buckshot shells for my rifle. I would then use the improvised ammunition to hunt birds around the Depot. I may have known my firearms from the inside out, but I was still pretty ignorant on bullet velocities fired from a weapon.

My friend, Greg from West Valley, would come spend time with me because we had remained best friends even after my move. One of the times that Greg came to stay with me, I showed him an improvised bullet I made from a large sewing pin. Whether I was thinking it would be funny, or just not thinking at all, I loaded the pin projectile in my rifle, aimed it at his buttocks, and pulled the trigger. The pin had a round, Mother of Pearl end that I expected to see sticking in Greg's butt. I thought we could all get a big laugh from this. Instead, the tip broke off, and the two-inch pin buried itself deep into his flesh. He instantly jumped in the air, grabbed his rear-end, and felt an intense burning in his ass cheek.

Greg was in a bad situation, and we knew our friendship would be in jeopardy if he decided to tell on me. We knew if he told the truth, his mom would not let us hang out anymore and neither of us wanted that. Richard and I had a two-story clubhouse we built in the back yard, so Greg had an idea. He told his mom that he fell off the clubhouse, and the pin that was buried in his butt was on our grass, and he landed on it. Everybody somehow believed him, and Greg and I were given the green light to continue being friends (after a small operation to remove the pin). He would have been better off telling his mom the truth, because his friendship with me was soon to put him in an even worse situation.

A mile south from our home on the Depot, there was an old, abandoned mining town, called Bauer. Richard and I discovered the place while skipping school one day. In 1981, there was an explosion somewhere in the town, which put an end to the small community there. I don't know if people were killed. I just recall the resulting fire from the explosion caused the town's abandonment. From the looks of the town, many teens from Tooele discovered this town long before us, and they used it as a party destination. There were about a dozen old houses and some buildings that appeared to be frozen in time. Whenever Richard and I went there, we found things from chemical canisters to dynamite blasting caps. We were teenagers with heavy firepower so, naturally, this became a favorite destination for us. Playing FBI agents, we kicked down the doors and fired into the abandoned houses at random, pretending to wipe out hoards of drug dealers.

Richard and I always had such a blast in this place, so we told my best friend about it. I made a quick phone call to Greg, and soon he arrived to see what we were talking about. After the short walk through the sagebrush field, Greg saw the town and loved the abandoned place as much as my brother and me. The three of us became rulers of this Old Ghost Town, and as far as we were concerned it was ours.

Bauer was a very unsafe place to hang out, and one time we walked into a building that had a laboratory in it. There we were, three kids with guns loaded to the nuts, staring at four walls lined with glass bottles. "Open fire!" was sounded, and after ten minutes and several re-loads later, there was not a whole bottle left in there. With a quick check to make sure glass was not embedded our flesh, we left the lab to explore some more. Upon leaving the building, a pheasant flew from the brush, and I shot it. I dressed the bird by a pond in the town using the pond's water to wash it. After building a fire, I cooked the poultry, and we ate it for lunch. We had no idea the water I'd just cleaned the bird in was filled with arsenic, but soon we would find that out.

On my fifteenth birthday, my dad bought me a 12-gauge shotgun. I wanted to break it in at the abandoned town. I wanted to camp out at the abandoned town with Greg and Richard, and Ted allowed us to do so. We jumped in our old Dodge van, and I drove to Bauer. I had no driver's license, but this never deterred my father from letting me drive.

A small paved road came off the main highway and led us into the town. There were not any "NO TRESPASSING" signs, only a gate with a stop sign on it at the entrance to the town. That didn't stop us. We drove around it from a short dirt road that bypassed the gate.

On the short drive we noticed something that was not there before, a large plume of smoke rising from the side of the road. It did not look like the typical smoke from a fire, but more like steam from a geyser. The rising smoke raised our curiosity, so we had to check it out. After parking the van in the circle at the end of town, we loaded our firearms and headed towards it.

Behind the town were giant tailing ponds where large amounts of chemicals were dumped. This is where the arsenic in the pond water, I cleaned the bird in earlier, came from. We were lucky it didn't make us sick, I guess. We made our way through the dried-up ponds, maneuvering over the small hills and valleys. After walking up the last hill, we looked down and saw a large crack in the ground, with a three-foot flame escaping it.

"Holy Shit!" all three of us yelled at the same time.

The Earth was on fire, and it looked like we walked into a volcano. I pointed my shotgun about six feet from where we stood and pulled the trigger. The buckshot hit the ground, and what looked like, lava started oozing out of it. Because I was the leader in our junior expedition, I walked closer to check out the substance flowing from the ground. A couple of feet from the molten ground, I started to sink, and my feet felt like they were on fire. I panicked, jumped out of it, and started to run. The rest of the party followed my lead and gave chase. Greg was right behind me, and my brother was to my left when it happened. Instead of taking the path that brought us in, I made a straight line for the closest solid ground I could see (big mistake). The ground opened up in front of me, like the "Gates of Hell", and I fell in. Greg was hot on my tail and saw what happened to me, and he tried to save me from it. His momentum sent him into the burning ground farther than I was, and he panicked. Richard was behind us and to our left, and he managed to escape without any injury. Greg and I were not so lucky, and we were caught in a large B-B-Q pit. My strong survival instincts finally kicked in, and I immediately threw my gun. Then I turned around to face the way I had entered that "hell hole". It was about a 4-foot rise to the lip of where I had fallen in, and I dug my arms in the ash and dirt, and I crawled out. I turned to see if I could help my friend, and I saw him clawing through the hot coals. I quickly jumped into my brother's footprints and made it to safety. Greg chose a different path than I had. He held onto his gun and dug his way through. He then moved up the burning hill, and the heat was intense as the hot coals were almost to his knees. Greg finally made it to a spot where I could help him, and I pulled him to safer ground. I looked at his hand and knew he was in trouble; the flesh on it looked like melted plastic, and he was going into shock.

I commanded Richard to go get the van parked at the end of town, and I stayed with Greg to comfort him. As soon as Richard arrived with the van, I raced home. Greg was crying out for his mother, and my feet were trembling on the gas and brake pedals due to my burns. We were both in shock by now, and I missed my driveway, parking the van in my backyard. I got Greg inside, laid him on the couch, and called the paramedics. Ted was not home. He had taken my little sister to the swimming pool, so he was not going to help us. The paramedics arrived a short time later and whisked us away to the hospital. As I was carried into the ambulance, a paramedic asked me how I felt, and responded my usual way. "I've had better days," I said immediately. "Even under these bad circumstances, I still had a sense of humor." I remember thinking.

My father didn't have health insurance for us, and I was terrified I would be in severe trouble with him. The first time I cried, that night, was when my father came to the hospital and saw me wrapped in bandages lying on a gurney.

"I'm sorry dad. I'm sorry we got hurt," I said to him with tears rolling down my face.

I think this was the first time in my life Ted actually comforted me, and he told me it would be all right.

I escaped major injury with my quick thinking and only ended up with second and third degree burns on my ankles. My friend, Greg was not as lucky, and he spent the next few months at The University of Utah Burn Center undergoing several operations and physical therapy.

We were on all of the local news programs, and there was talk of a lawsuit. One of the reporters from the local newspaper wrote an article about the incident and hardly got any of the story right. There was another article about the City suing the company who owned the property for a figure around 8 million dollars to clean up the waste. I don't know what came of that; I just remember thinking that if the city could sue for that amount, "I was going to be rich."

That was not the case, but my dad got together with Greg's parents to file a lawsuit in an attempt to get some money for this tragedy. We could have taken the property owners to the cleaners, but from what I recollect, Ted got greedy, and we lost lawyers.

I did not even get a phone call or a get-well card from my mother. Now, wouldn't you think with this traumatic event happening to her youngest boys, she would have been by our sides? In fact, I was not even sure where my mother was.

While I was convalescing from my accident, the phone rang and there was a woman on the other line. It was a lady that worked with one of my dad's brothers. My uncle set up a blind date for my dad and this woman. Part of my conversation with her, included how she had a daughter my age who was a real, "Looker." Well that was all I needed to hear, and I gave my father their number.

A date was set up for Ted and that woman, her name was Angie, and soon their whirlwind romance developed. After a month of dating, the two wanted to get married. Ted and Angie were hitched in a Mormon church without any major fan-fair. While they were dating, her daughter, Heather and I discovered young love, and we began a relationship as well.

With Ted and Angie now legally man and wife, we had to move again. We left the Army Depot and moved into Angie's big house in Bountiful, Utah. Angie had five children, and my oldest brother Brad moved back with us, so with our five family members and her six, the head count at the house was up to eleven. The house was full and every room that could hold somebody did. Her daughter and I shared a room together, and neither parent cared.

Pre-marital sex is a big "no-no" with the Mormons, so my attempts to consummate our step-sibling relationship failed for several months.

Angie was a nurse working a graveyard shift, and Ted worked at the Depot during the day. While Ted worked, Angie slept, and we children raised hell however we could.

My father's new wife had a Pontiac Firebird. I thought that car was hot, and I got behind the wheel of it often. In fact, this car and Angie's home were the main reasons Ted married her, I remember him telling me. I drove the streets of Bountiful at high rates of speed and managed to tear up a few lawns along the way. Angie thought the car was a waste, and it was sold shortly after she married my dad, but not until I beat the crap out of it for a couple of weeks, and almost killed my brother and myself in it.

After the car was sold, I wanted a motorcycle, and it was not long before I got one.

Angie was easily manipulated, and I took advantage of that. Usually just by telling her I wanted something, I got it. Without anyone's permission, I looked in the newspaper and found a used motorcycle for sale. I took the paper to my step-mom and simply told her to give me the two hundred dollars required to get it. Without much hesitation, Brad drove me, in our old Dodge van, to pick up the motorcycle. I took it for a quick test drive, and then I gave the owner the money, and we put the bike in the back of the van and headed home.

Driving home, I remember Brad was playing like he was a racecar driver from the popular game, at the time, "Pole Position" while he drove. The stress of treating our van like an "Indy" car in a video game meant, "Game Over" for the old van, and we were stranded on the freeway. My brother pulled over as the smoke billowed from the engine, and the old girl coasted to a stop. Over the years we had put that thing through its paces, and I was sad to see her die like that. I took charge of the situation without waiting for help and asked for the keys to the car that was back at the house. I pulled my newly acquired motorcycle from the van, kicked started it to life, and raced down the side of the freeway. With a light-less motorcycle, I made my way up the dark streets, through a couple of stoplights, and reached the house without any incident. I garaged the bike, jumped in the car, and made the rescue.

I was a "holy terror" on this motorcycle Angie bought for me, and I never cared whose property I damaged along the way. I rode the motorcycle in Angie's backyard and did donuts all over it, destroying the grass in the process. Nobody seemed to care about my cool grass circles, and I grew bored with that, so I started driving it in the dirt where it belonged. I drove the bike to some hills that were close to the house. I was not familiar with the area, but I felt pretty confident about my riding skills. Riding around the dirt a short time, I spied some other people near a hill climbing it with

56

their bikes. As you might expect, I rode over to check it out. They were smoking weed and climbing the steep hill. One guy asked what kind of bike I had, and I told him, "It's a Suzuki 250."

"Oh you'll have no problem climbing that hill," he said.

"No I'd better not," I said, unsure of my climbing ability.

He then offered me a toke off his pipe, and I stupidly accepted. Not staying much longer, I fired up my bike and took off. I sped down a trail that I had not been down yet. I was going fast to show off. As I went around a corner, my speed was about forty mph when I noticed that the trail passed over a twelve-foot wide wash. The wash was at least eight feet deep, and it was only twenty feet away from me. With no time to brake, I made a command decision to "gas" the bike and try to "Evil Kenevel" my way across it. I am sure it didn't help to have my brain baked to a golden-brown, from the pot I smoked earlier. I made it most of the way across the wash, until my front tire embedded into the lip on the other side, instantly stopping the bike. I kept moving, however, and my tender testicles implanted themselves on the metal gas tank. All the air was knocked out of me, and I fell to the ground. My motorcycle made it across the wash, but it sustained some damage. The people I had been talking with turned to see where the loud thud came from, and they saw me pulling myself off the ground. It felt like I got hit in the crotch with a sledgehammer, and I thought blood was pouring from my traumatized sack. I did not care who was watching, as I pulled my pants down, to assess the damage.

"Good no blood," I thought. I pulled my pants back up, and gingerly walked to my motorcycle. "What went wrong?" I wondered. This was the familiar stunt I practiced for all those years ago on my bicycle. Nobody tried to help me, and I felt pretty stupid for my failed stunt. I picked up my bike and made a quick look at the damage to my motorcycle. There was a dent on the gas tank where my "boys" met the metal. The forks of the bike were bent, and my handlebars were tweaked. She did not look good, but started right up. I rode her sidesaddle back home in an attempt to coddle the damaged, elite region of my body.

The motorcycle was wrecked, and I had no money to fix it, so I didn't want to keep it anymore. I walked the motorcycle about two miles to my friend's house to try and barter for some drugs. He was not home, and I did not want to walk it back up the hill to my house. His bedroom window was open, and it appeared to be a good spot to enter. I climbed through his window and helped myself to a couple of ounces of his weed. I grabbed what I thought was a fair amount for the wrecked bike, and I walked home with a big sack of weed in my pocket. He had no clue his drugs were gone because of the large amount in his house. Later, I told him he could have the motorcycle, free of charge. (Gee, wasn't that nice of me?)

Behind Angie's house was a small camping trailer. We never used the trailer for camping in the mountains, but we managed to give it plenty of use. We hellions filled it with pot smoke and heavy metal music. Some friends of mine who were supposed to be in school, instead, sluffed in the trailer with me. We had the marijuana I took in place of my bike, and smoked it in a homemade bong.

I did not know my father was home, and I was probably too stoned to care. In mid-bong hit, the trailer door swung open, and my father was smacked in the face by a cloud of smoke. He immediately called my friends bad names, and his face color turned the usual, "Fire Engine Red." I knew at that point I was in some "deep shit".

My father told my friends to, "Get the fuck home," and stormed out of the trailer.

I cannot explain what happened inside of me, but I snapped. I was sixteen years old, and found myself bigger than the man that kicked my ass for so many years. Somehow, I stood up and was hot on his tail. I threw the trailer door open before it had finished closing from him leaving, and I screamed at him to apologize to my friends. He didn't take too kindly to that. He turned around to face me, and the fight was on. I tucked my head down and bull-charged him, smacking him in the chest with my head and pushing away with my arms. He was instantly knocked to the ground and looked completely stunned from what I had just done. I too was in shock, and I felt an enormous amount of power. There was an old trampoline in the back of our yard and I was standing right by it. When he stood up to charge me, I had already anticipated his move. I ducked my head again, and wrapped my arms around his torso. There I was, a sixteen year old, holding my dad like he was a big baby needing to be burped. He was not though, so I threw him as hard as I could against the steel bars of the trampoline (where there should have been padding). I watched his body contort to the odd-shaped trampoline bars, and a big rush of air escaped from his lungs. He fell to the ground and was out of breath.

I went and stood over him, "You've kicked my ass long enough!" I said to him with my, newly found, braveness. I bent down and got right in his face, with more to say. "Touch me again, and I'll kill you," I casually told him. I understand that sounds a little harsh, but my whole life to this point was all one sided and brutal, with him. Suddenly, I felt like I did not have to take it anymore. I beat him soundly and knew his ability to control me, physically was over.

Ted and Angie were doing poor as a couple, and it was very early in their marriage. She was not use to the level of violence he brought with him to the relationship, and I figured they would not last much longer. For some reason, though Ted and Angie sold the house in Bountiful and purchased another home in Tooele, and we had to move back.

I was three years into my teens, and my established independence, combined with my youth, was a cocktail of trouble.

CHAPTER FIVE:
CONFINE THE ANIMALS

My mom was out of my life now for over two years, and I continued wondering where she was, and how she was doing.

Ted's wife was nice enough to me; I just wasn't sure how to respect her. When Ted was at work, most of us found it quite easy to walk all over Angie, so we did. My father did not teach me how to treat women right, or other people, for that matter. I was ignorant in the respect department, but I figured since I was not beating up women or children, I must be a good guy.

Heather and I were doing better, as a couple, than our parents were, and the relationship with my step-sister/girlfriend was moving along okay. We had been going out for six months when we moved back to Tooele, and the most drama in our relationship was from me slicing up my arms with a razor blade, to get some attention from her. Reflecting back, the way I learned to get something positive, was through a negative action. I was never taught how to deal with emotions from either of my parents.

Because Heather and I were left to our own devices, un-parented, we hastily fell in love. Of course, I had no understanding about real love. I confused the lust I felt for love. We were way off the map, and clueless to our eventual downfall, but talked of marriage, anyway. I used the prospect of our future wedding to my advantage, and finally talked her into having sex with me. Heather was concerned about having sex under the same roof as our parents, so all we needed was a place to go to express our juvenile love. One of our next-door neighbors had a big camping trailer on the side of their home, and with some careful breaking and entering, we had a love nest. Once we started having sex, it became a daily pastime. The sex gave us a stronger feeling of love, and our relationship temporarily grew.

By sixteen, my street survival skills were well established. Fear of my father's physical abuse was not much of an issue for me anymore. He knew he could no longer control me with violence and just, "kicked back" to let me ruin my life. Richard and I, along with one of his friends, started breaking into houses and ripping people off. We were arrogant little punks on individual paths of self-destruction. Selfishly, we hurt other people for our own gain and loved every minute of it. At this moment in my life, all the pieces formed to shape me into a criminal. There was no obtainable concept in my mind that my actions were affecting others. As long as I was taking care of my needs, nothing or no one mattered. With our move back to Tooele and a new girlfriend, I tried to go to school again. I always struggled in school and never fit in. I was more content on acting the fool, and depending on the situation, this could be a good thing or bad. The majority of the time humor brought me comfort, but sometimes it brought me trouble.

I recall a male schoolmate, whose girlfriend started to take a fancy to me (it must have been my rugged good looks and quick whit). One time he caught her batting her eyes at me, and he took it upon himself to kick my ass.

"What the Hell did I do?" "She approached me and initiated our conversations," I tried to explain.

He confronted me in the hallway after school, and did not give me a chance to defend myself verbally. He started pounding me. The guy was bigger than me and had a decisive edge, and he got the better of the fight. After the short scuffle, a teacher broke it up and sent us on our way. I was "pissed-off" at him and figured the best way to get back at him was to burglarize his house. I told Richard and his friend of my plan to rob him, and they went along with it and helped me. I found out where he lived, and the next day we ditched school to raid his home. With a fast entry from a back window, three wild teens were on the loose in his room. I don't remember exactly what we grabbed, but the items filled our arms with loot. We left his house, and walked down the middle of the street, in broad daylight, with our stash of stolen goods.

My delinquent, street-survival skills that were already established at sixteen enabled me to get money for marijuana and alcohol purchases. I began showing up at the pawnshop with my eighteen-year-old drug dealer. And he helped me fence "the goods" that were stolen. He got to keep the majority of the cash, but he gave me a little weed and beer money. Everything was working out fine, until the day I wanted more. My robbery attempts evolved, and soon the drug dealer was not safe from me any more. On a whim, Richard, his friend, and I thought it would be challenging to rob our drug dealer. I had broke into a dealer's house before this, and got away with it, so I felt pretty confident it could be done this time also. We had a system already established, and if we were unclear of the home's occupancy, one of us would ring the doorbell or knock to see if someone would answer. If someone answered the door, we would simply ask, "If they knew where somebody's house was."

It was a beautiful day in the neighborhood, when the crime went down. We made the short journey to our dealer's house at about 11:00 in the AM. He lived with his mother, and we knew she was working, but we thought he was at a friend's house, partying. We found ourselves at the front door wondering if we should commit the crime. I made the decision to proceed with the caper, and Richard and his friend agreed with it. We rang the doorbell and beat on the door, as loud as we could, for several minutes. No one answered, so we felt it was safe to go inside. We tried to open the front door, but it was locked, so an alternate plan was needed. I walked around the side of their house and noticed the kitchen window was out of sight from other houses. I did not care about the noise it would make, and I smashed the window. With a small boost up, I was inside opening the front door for the rest of the gang. We tore through the small living room in a couple of minutes, looking for anything of value. Right off the bat, we had a four-foot water bong and a good-sized bag of weed. That was not enough for us, so I made my way down the hall and into his bedroom. As soon as I opened his door, I found him lying in his bed, just waking up. We both had a look of complete shock, as we stared at each other. All I could do was turn and run, as I warned my two other accomplices. "Get the fuck out of here, he's home!" I screamed in a panic. While I yelled my warning, we all scooped up what we could and sprinted out the door and ran home. I lived in fear for a few days; because I heard rumors he was going to kick my ass, but when I ran into him at a party later, he did nothing to me. He was not the meanest guy around, and I must have scared the crap out of him when he woke-up, the day I robbed him and stood above him.

I burned my bridge with my drug dealer/friend, so I began to search for new ones. At Tooele High, I made two new friends, Dan and Jeff, and we all started to hang out together. With these people, I was in my comfort zone. It was the usual situation with me, as with the other friends in my life. Dan's Parents were not in his life (for reasons I cannot remember), but he lived with his cousin. Jeff's parents were divorced, and he lived with his alcoholic father, so his house is where we spent a lot of our time. Jeff's dad worked during the day, but afterward he could be found in one place, "Red's Bar."

As usual, we were left to do as we pleased, and drinking and partying was our main pastime. Before we could begin drinking, sometimes we would stand in front of the 7-11, waiting for the right person to buy us beer.

"Hey man will you buy us some beer," Dan would ask.

Dan was a people person and could usually get what he asked for. Sometimes it worked on the first try, other times he would have to ask a few different people, but we always eventually got our beer. Remember this, friends, children can get anything they ask for if they ask the wrong people. I spent plenty of time at Jeff's house partying the night away. When I finally made my way home from Jeff's house, Ted never questioned my whereabouts.

Ted was unloading huge piles of shit on his life and relationships because he was so miserable. My father was burdened by torment, and it disabled him. I think since he could no longer beat his children up like before, he focused his rage on Angie. I would come home at times, walk past their bedroom, and hear the old familiar sound of a woman getting thumped-on. I had some thoughts of wanting to help her, but also felt that the next time I fought my dad, I would want to kill him. I decided avoiding Ted, like the plague, when he was in his violent moods was best for both of us.

My friend Dan had his driver's license, but no car. Ted had a Ford Escort station wagon, and we talked him into letting us drive it. I guess my dad figured because Dan had his license, he was responsible enough to use the car. He was driving us all around Tooele, and introducing us to a new level of stunts.

About a mile out of town, Dan took us to an old highway with railroad tracks intersecting it. The tracks were situated with the lower part of the road rising up to meet the tracks, creating a man-made ramp. This made a perfect car jump, and Ted's car would be tested like no Ford Escort had been before. Dan started hitting the tracks between forty and fifty mph. At that speed the car would catch a little air, but it was not enough for us. Soon, Dan had the speedometer reading between sixty and seventy mph, and the little car caught serious air. Richard and I wanted to look at this marvelous event from outside the car, so Dan dropped us off on the side of the highway. Dan drove the car back down the road, turned around, and hit the gas. Richard and I stood a couple of feet off the road as the car approached us at sixty-five mph. When Dan hit the tracks at that high speed, the Escort launched into the air. It went five feet skyward and flew thirty feet down the asphalt. The tracks were perfect for this, and every jump ended with a four-point landing.

We jumped the car at least six times; until we got scared the wheels would fall off. From what we could see, the sturdy little Ford was no worse-for-wear. Ted never caught on to the thrashings his car was subjected to, so we continued driving it.

One night while Dan and I drove around the Tooele neighborhoods, he took me by a cop's house. He mentioned to me how he didn't care for the police officer, so I sought to help Dan, however I could.

"Pull over up here, and I'll slash his tires," I gratefully offered.

Dan dropped me off, up the road from the officer's house. I ran to the police car with a small pocketknife; opened it up, and punctured two of the tires. The "hiss" from the escaping air was pretty loud. I ran back to the get-away car as fast as possible. The cop car was temporarily immobilized, and we hurried out of there. With that, we still did not have enough fun, and we went to find another police vehicle. By the time our night ended, two police officers would wake up to flattened tires the next morning. Dan and I had some fun, and I put the event out of my head. I was not operating on cognizant thought. **My actions were controlled by ignorance, and a sub-conscious need to ruin myself.**

I continued my path of destruction. With five dollars, some trash, and my father's red truck, we got Ted arrested at his job, and he was at his limit with us. The story begins with Ted wanting us to do a driving chore for him. None of his three younger children had driver's licenses, but this never stopped our dad from letting us drive. He was a driver's education teacher since I was at least five, and from that age on, I had a steering wheel in my hand. When my friend, Dan was not available to drive, Richard and

I would get the call from my father. We drove a lot for our dad and ran his errands frequently.

One Saturday, Richard and I were instructed by Ted to take a load of garbage in his small red truck to the dump. He gave us five dollars to pay the dump fee, and then he went to work. With an "Abe Lincoln" in our hand, we figured a five-dollar bag of weed would do us much better than paying any dump fee. We still needed a place to get rid of the trash, however, and since we were in Tooele, there was plenty of open space to dump the waste.

We found a dirt road and followed it for about a mile, until we thought it was safe to dump the load. We stopped the truck, pulled the garbage off, and then drove away, thinking we just got one over on the county landfill. We were carefree until Monday, and that's when our stupidity caught up to us. Ted was at his security job on the Depot, when the Tooele City Police showed up and arrested him in front of all his colleagues. Ted told us later, the officers were not very kind to him either.

Apparently, the land we dumped the trash on belonged to Festus Haggen, from the popular television show "Gunsmoke." I had no idea this guy lived in Utah, let alone in Tooele. He was, understandably, not happy with the truckload of trash on his land and wanted the perpetrators caught. With a little detective work, the trash was combed through, and my dad's name and address were found on an old bill in the, illegally dumped, waste.

Richard and I heard about our father's predicament from one of Angie's kids. We decided being home with Ted that evening was not the healthiest place to be, so we ran away to Dan's house for a day. We came back home the next day and Ted had cooled down, but I could tell he was frustrated and had enough from his two youngest sons.

Richard and I avoided our father and he returned the favor to us. We hardly said anything to him, and we continued with our business. Our business was stealing from people and raising hell. We were crooked people, and when we desired something, it was easily ours.

My brother and I were way out of control with a feeling of invincibility from our father and the police. Our major trouble with the law came to a head when we stole from a truck parked by the High School swimming pool. We peeked in the window and saw a pack of cigars sitting on the dash. The doors were locked, but with a push on the side window, my hand was able to squeeze in and grab the cigars. The truck belonged to the school maintenance worker, and he watched us break into his truck. He called the police when we walked behind the school, and over to the football field. Richard, myself, and two of our friends had just started smoking some marijuana, when a policeman came around the brick building we stood by, and he arrested us. We were taken to the police station and interrogated separately. The other kids got to go ahead of Richard and me, so we had to sit and wait while the detectives talked to them. I started to get frustrated from waiting there so long, and it caused me to get lippy.

"You guys can't keep us here this long without charging us with something," I bold-fully said.

I got up to leave, and the officer commanded me to, "Sit back down!" That was about the time I knew how much trouble I was in. After some hours sitting there, they called Richard and I in and gave us the bad news.

"We just sat your friends down and got them to tell us everything," the Detective said. "Now we want to hear your side of it," he calmly said to me.

Richard and I started singing like a couple of canaries. I confessed to everything, from the house robberies, to the cop-tire vandalism. My tire slashing stupidity must have been a bonus to them because of the look on the Detectives' faces when I told them.

"Oh, you did that," he said.

"Shit," I thought. "I'm giving out to much information here."

The Tooele Police printed out my "rap" sheet. In less than a year, it had grown to twenty separate crimes, fifteen of which were felonies.

After several hours at the station, our dad was called. The officers asked Ted if he was going to come and get us, and he told them, "No." He was beyond tired of dealing with Richard and me, and left us for the courts to handle. At midnight, a Sheriff took us fifty miles into Salt Lake, to the Juvenile Detention Center.

We were locked-up for a week before our court hearing. The Judge looked at our long list of charges and sentenced us to thirty days in detention. I thought it was excessive, but what did I know? After all, I was the "poster child" of bad circumstance. As far as I was concerned, my *fucked-up* parents put me in this situation.

Shortly prior to Christmas time that year, my brother and I were in court trying to get a break in our sentence so we could spend 48-hours with our Family. The Judge ruled that we could go home for the holiday, and we were released into our father's custody. As soon as we got home, Richard and I hooked-up with his old friend that we had been in trouble with before. The two of them decided to break into a house to steal some Christmas presents. I didn't join them in the burglary because I felt that I was in enough trouble at that point. They found a home that was unoccupied, broke-in, and stole some presents from under the Christmas tree. I waited for them out in the street, so I guess you could call me an accomplice. They took a radar-detector and a coin-separator filled with money, and then met me back on the street. I lightly cursed them out as we walked down the sidewalk, and we went our separate ways. I made it back home without getting busted for another robbery, and I spent the rest of my short vacation with Heather.

After our small Christmas break, we went back to Detention. I did not like having my freedom taken from me. It had always been easy for me to look at outside situations and evaluate them pretty well, but when it came to my own situations, I had a difficult time accepting responsibility for my actions. It was easier for me to put the blame squarely on my parent's shoulders, and act as I saw fit. **Now, I was realizing that I needed to look at where I was, and how I got there. I made a little progress on my self-discovery, but I had a long way to go.**

Our thirty-day sentence finally ended, and I was excited to go home. However, Ted was still enjoying his freedom from us and was not ready to let us come back home. With our father no longer wanting us, the Courts moved us from the Detention center to a lock- down house called, "Extended Shelter." The shelter was filled with about a dozen losers just like us. And it's easily described by calling it a "juvenile halfway house". We were locked in here, but sometimes we got to do certain activities with counselor supervision. It was winter, so our main activities were skiing and, as usual, using drugs.

I encountered more drugs in that shelter than I had ever seen before. Seasickness pills were the rage in the shelter, and we stole Merazines from K-MART whenever we got to breathe fresh air. With twelve to a box, one box of them would cause serious hallucinations, and the little white pills were everywhere in the home. The head-trips from the pills were intense, but the way they made my body feel was very un-comfortable. I tried the pills about four different times until concluding they were not for me.

Richard and I spent about a month and a half in this so called "Shelter." And I was, now, more of a criminal than when I went in. When we had to leave the shelter, we went to Youth Services because Ted was still "basking in the sun" on the vacation he took from us. Youth Services was a few miles from the Detention Facility and the Extended Shelter, so I kind of felt like I was getting somewhere. I was not, evidently, and found myself scheming and manipulating my way through there.

Youth Services was a minimum-security building just off of Main Street, in Salt Lake City. It was a co-ed facility with about 30 teens inside. Each room held eight people, and the windows in the rooms had cheap alarms on them. With a quick distraction of the counselor behind the desk, we could shut off the main alarm, and then disable the alarms on the windows. We took apart the magnetic alarms and jumped the wires inside to bypass the alarm. Another small distraction of the counselor would enable us to turn the alarm back on, and the counselor was oblivious of our plan to escape. By pulling a "MacGyver" on our windows, the freedom was there for us to come and go as we pleased. Our destination was usually the supermarket behind Youth Services to steal cigarettes and rolling papers. My sneakiness only lasted until I was busted by one of the counselors, while I was smoking a joint as I leaned out the window. It was at the end of our stay here when this happened, and Ted only allowed Richard home, and not me because of the joint infraction. I was sent off to a place called ARTEC (Adolescent Rehabilitation Training and Education Center), if I remember correctly.

From the start, ARTEC was better than the other places I had just gone through. At the time, ARTEC was in an old building on State Street and 2100 South, in SLC. On the bottom floor were our rooms, and only two kids at a time stayed in each. It felt nice for me to finally be able to stretch my legs and not feel so cramped. ARTEC was the only adolescent facility in Utah where under-aged teens were allowed to smoke. It is hard for me to believe, to this day, but all we had to do was go into the bathroom to smoke our little lungs away. There were even smoking chairs set up in the bathrooms and some ashtrays for us.

ARTEC's program was structured to start out on level one, and I had to work my way to level five, in order to eventually graduate. How quickly I got through the program, depended on how I behaved, and what I learned. At first, I did not behave too well or learn too much. I mostly tried to get through by remaining pig-headed and ignorant. Counseling and Education were the staples of ARTEC, so I had to "straighten up" and "fly-right", if I wanted to get out of there.

Heather visited me on several occasions during my stays in the different lock-up facilities, and it had been several months without physical contact from my girlfriend because it wasn't allowed while I was detained. I wanted to be alone with her.

My sister, Rachel was getting married while I was locked up, and I used her wedding for an excuse to see Heather. I was at level three in ARTEC by now, but had not earned enough privileges to get out for my sister's wedding. I called Heather and told her I had a plan to escape. She liked it, and she helped me bust out. It was a lock-down facility at night, but during the day we were free to go outdoors for short periods at a time.

Heather got a ride from her friend in Tooele, and they met me in front of ARTEC. I walked outside pretending to go play "Hackey Sack," jumped in the car, and split. I was AWOL, but I did not care because I was free.

I had a lot of fun at Rachel's wedding, and I finally got to spend some time alone with my girlfriend. I was "on the run" for about a week before Ted and Angie talked me into going back and finishing my sentence.

Arriving back at ARTEC, I was dropped to level one and had to start all over again. I was tired of feeling like a caged animal by now, and I would rather be free.

Up to this point my academic grades suffered throughout my life. I barely skated by in school, and the counselors were about to find that out. As they looked at my transcripts, they saw it plastered with D's and F's, and they challenged me to do better. I was never encouraged to do well in school before, and I never had anyone to help me with homework, but I accepted their challenge. I decided to "buckle down" and see what I could do.

I was fresh into the eleventh grade, and thanks to ARTEC, I was in a small class where I received the attention I needed. When my grades came, at the end of the quarter, I was shocked; "3.9 GPA", and I did not even break a sweat. **I began to see something in me that went unnoticed before. If I applied my mind to something, I could easily achieve it.** I put the rest of my time at ARTEC on cruise control, and after six months, I was "free" again. Ted was still not ready to accept me into his home, so off to a foster home I went.

CHAPTER SIX:
ANIMAL INSTINCTS

After being married for less than a year, Ted's abuse drove Angie to counseling, and the therapist told her my dad was a schizophrenic. I remember Angie relaying this information about my Dad's mental health to me, and I did not find it shocking. Angie and I talked quite a bit, and as we did, I pondered my past with Ted. I thought what her therapist said about my father made a tremendous amount of sense. My dad had at least three different personalities that I could count: the raging psychopath who beat women and children, the sad man who was too depressed to function, and the happy-go-lucky man who could joke and laugh with the best of them. I think Wanda shares these same traits, except she didn't abuse people, physically; instead my mom had the ability to wreck someone mentally. Soon after Angie started therapy, her relationship with my father came to an end.

Angie and the rest of her family moved into a duplex down the road from our broken home, and then she annulled their marriage. Ted lived at the duplex with Angie for a month or so until their house was sold, and he could find a new place. I lived in a foster home in the Salt Lake Valley, and Heather lived at home with her mother. I worked out ways to get rides to see Heather, and we spent as much time as we could together. I had a lot of catching up to do with my girlfriend, and that meant to me, we had to have sex every chance we could. At that time I thought we were mature enough to have children. Now looking back, I know this was a very stupid thing for me to think, but my brain thrived off stupidity, and I was filled with it.

My thinking was simplistic, "If I was going to spend my life with this girl, let's seal the deal with a child."

We made several attempts with no luck and it began to wear on us, but mostly on Heather. We did not have a vehicle, and I had no intention of getting a job. After any missed period, Heather would walk from her house to a clinic in Tooele to take a pregnancy test. "No," was the answer every time, and we began to talk about what could be wrong. She put the blame on me; and in return, I would put it back on her. This caused some friction between us, and our relationship suffered. Heather eventually moved from Tooele into her cousin's home in Centerville, Utah. Ted found a rundown apartment in West Valley, where He, LouRee, Richard and our old family dog, Natasha moved into.

On my seventeenth birthday, Ted invited me to his apartment to celebrate. He bought me a big cake and set it on the table of the dining room until I arrived. Natasha could not wait for the celebration. She jumped on the table and ate her fill of the cake. Ted came home and saw what she did, and then tore into her. When I got to the apartment, my sister Rachel told me what happened, and I saw the tattered cake. I didn't care anything about the ruined pastry, but I was upset at my dad for beating Natasha. She was my dog, and for what I cared; she could have eaten as much of the cake as she wanted. I was angry with Ted for abusing Natasha over something so trivial, and my feelings towards him subdued the birthday celebration. Ted was a walking piece of broccoli, and he was barely there mentally. By now, you understand he was never there as a parent, but we could have probably poked him in the eye with a stick at this point, and he wouldn't have felt it. My dad's functions were limited to work and staying home. After getting home from work he either slept or drooled on himself in front of the television. Ted was severely depressed, and the only thing he was providing my two younger siblings; was a roof over their head, and that roof, as usual, was surrounded by a lot of bad people. My dad was the type of person who did not believe in medical help, and probably did not want to admit that he had mental health issues. I could tell my dad needed help, but was clueless on how to get him that help. These were tough times for Richard, LouRee, and myself, and our mother had completely disappeared from our lives. I felt she did not care anything about us.

Being a teenager, the only staples I needed in my life were; sex, drugs, and rock and roll. Richard and I made many friends around my dad's apartment complex, and it seemed everyone used drugs. We could start at one end of the complex and by the time we reached the other end, have sampled almost any drug available. Luckily, we stayed away from the heavy stuff. Weed and beer gave us what we looked for in drugs. So we didn't experiment with the real bad mind-benders.

Richard had a serious girlfriend, whose friend lived in the same apartment complex as he did. And the two spent a lot of time at their mutual friend's apartment. Through Richard, Ted became friends with the woman that lived there also. They decided the apartments were not the best place to live anymore, and I think my dad liked her. Ted and her combined their resources and rented a house in Taylorsville a few miles south.

I was doing all right at my foster home for a little while. I was just not comfortable there. Heather began to lose interest in me, and I worried she was going to break-up with me. People in her family told Heather I was a loser. Not surprisingly, they were right, and it caused Heather to want someone better. She gave me the talk of separating for a while to figure things out, and I was not taking it very well. Through my life, I developed serious abandonment issues, but I had no idea how to deal with them. I hatched an idea to win back her favor; and it included me chopping off one of my digits to keep her ("Holy Van Gogh's Batman"). I concluded the pinky on my left hand was the least valuable to me, so it would be the one that would go. In the garage of my foster home, I laid my poor finger down on the wood table, and I prepared to remove it. I raised the small hatchet, and read the last rights to my finger, before finally coming to my senses and deciding not to see it go. Sure, it was just a little finger, but it was mine, I wanted it. I put down the hatchet and realized that what I *was* going to do was *super-dumb*. I gave Heather some space and that worked in its place, go figure. Heather and I were back on track a short time later, and I was grateful to have all ten fingers.

My dad and I started communicating on a small, but effective level, and he finally heard me say, "I want to come home." My foster family was receiving over 400 dollars a month from me being there so they wanted to keep me, but because I was barely seventeen when Ted let me go home, my foster family had no say in the matter.

I still didn't have my driver's license due to my time in the system, and, as in the past, this minor detail didn't stop Ted from letting me drive. He let me use his truck, so I could move my things from my foster home to the shared home in Taylorsville. At the foster home, I backed the small truck up in the driveway and tried to load it as fast as possible. If somebody saw what I was doing, there would be trouble. Sure enough, my foster brother spotted me as I loaded the last box, and he tried to stop me. I jumped in the truck and started it. He told me not to leave until I talked to his mom. He tried to grab a box from the truck. I slammed the truck in gear, and I "flipped him off" with my middle finger as I sped out of the driveway. There was one problem I need to mention; his friend's car was parked on the side of the long driveway, and as I was "flipping him off", I looked in the side-mirror of the truck to see his expression from my finger, and the skid-marks I left. I paid too much attention to him, and not to where I was going. I sideswiped the car in the driveway, and then I got scared and split out of there as fast as I could. "Bam," not even moved back home yet, and I already had a hit and run.

In the past year, I matured somewhat, so after I got home, I called the police to turn myself in for the accident. I was in juvenile Court once again, and I tried to blame the accident on my father. With Ted sitting right by me, I explained how my dad *made me* drive the truck. I also told the judge about the many driving errands he tasked me with over the years. **I was still playing a victim, trying to put the blame elsewhere.** The Judge did not buy it, and he explained to me that since I was driving, it was my fault.

"Huh, that makes sense," I thought.

Because I called and turned myself in, the Judge went easy on me. I had to do a little community service and pay some restitution, but that was a lot better than getting locked-up again. I was on my way to being an adult, and I could not blame my parents for my stupid actions much longer. I did try to have a couple of conversations with Ted about how I was raised by him and Wanda, and how my upbringing was causing me to act out, but he never bought it and continued to argue that I was in control of my own actions. By now, I did agree with him, to a certain extent, but I thought there had to be some validity to what I was saying.

I was back at home, and from the things I went through, a sense of who I was began emerging. I never wanted trouble with the law, but still was not taking all the steps necessary to avoid it. I completely dropped out of school by now because I figured it was just not for me. Public school was like a different planet to me, and I did not have a support system to cope with it. I realized I was not completely stupid, and I knew that there was some creative intellect to me. My parents just happened to be retarded when it came time to show love or encouragement to their children, and we suffered "big time" for this.

Richard and I now got away with everything right in front of our dad. The house we lived in had a greenhouse off the back. We came to the conclusion one day that growing pot would be a fun activity. Ted came home and noticed a plant in the greenhouse, looking a little odd as it stretched its leaves in the mid-day sun.

"What is that," he asked Richard and me.

"It's a tomato plant," I sarcastically said. For a brief second I thought we were in trouble, until he replied "Yeah right."

"I don't want that shit in the house," he said, as he walked downstairs.

Richard and I let it grow for a couple of more days until we decided it would do us better rolled in some paper, and then the little plant was gone.

My brother and I partied all the time, but neither of us had a job to pay for beer. Our creative minds could easily solve most of our problems, and we wanted to avoid any trouble with the police, so instead of stealing from strangers, we began to "rip off" our father. Richard went through some of Ted's papers and found the PIN number to his savings account. While our dad slept at night, Richard would sneak into his room and take the card whenever he needed some extra cash. Richard gave me the number once, and I used it to take sixty dollars for some stupid reason. I told Richard how much I took, and he got upset with me.

"You're going to get us busted," he said. "Stop taking so much at a time," he lectured.

"Well, if that wasn't the pot calling the kettle black" I thought, and I stopped taking the card. I think my brother still used it after that, however, I don't know if our dad ever caught on to the thievery. Richard stole quite a bit from him.

The lady who shared our house with us lived in the up stairs part, and we stayed in the basement. Our shared living connection only worked out well for about a month. After that, she and Ted started butting heads. Initially, my dad liked her, but that quickly changed because she had homosexual friends. It was odd to me that my father disliked her friends so much. My older brother, Brad is gay. He "came out of the closet" about this time; Ted was devastated by the news of his son's sexual preference, but he still seemed to accept it. For some reason, though, he could not accept it with other homosexuals, in fact, he seemed almost afraid of them. Because of all the static around our home, and like clockwork; we had to move again. We moved back up north to a condo Ted bought in Centerville, Utah. It was a large three-bedroom condominium on the third floor of the complex. This new place was a move up from the "shit holes" we had lived in over the past several years, and I didn't mind this move because it put me closer to Heather.

Thanks to many years of moving, I easily established myself in this small Mormon community. I seemed to make friends with the same type of people, and I made a friend in the complex that we moved into. Matt was his name, and I am sure it was no coincidence that we enjoyed the same activities. Getting drunk was the norm for us, and that was about all we did.

Ted began to date a woman who was originally from Mudlake, Idaho, and they made a three-hour drive there almost every weekend. It left the condo in our complete control, and we felt like it was ours to keep. We kept our usual party activities, and had a good time doing them. The good feelings continued, when our phone rang and on the other line was a voice I had not heard in a very long time.

"Hi mom," I said. "What's been going on?" I asked her.

She told me she'd met a guy, and he was "special" to her. Richard, LouRee and I were invited to Wanda's apartment in Salt Lake City, to meet her "special guy". Our mom made a fine batch of home made waffles, and we sat down for breakfast with her as she introduced us to her new friend, Brian Mitchell. We ate the tasty breakfast and listened to Mitchell's babble as long as we could stand it. Then Richard and I went outside to smoke a cigarette, and we commented on Wanda's new love.

"That guy is a *fuck'n wacko*," we said almost in unison.

Through the years and situations I had survived, I seemed to have developed a sixth sense in regards to evaluating people. I guess most people who survive abuse, develop this sort of sense and can read people like books. I don't remember much of my conversation with Mitchell. I just know my initial feelings of him were extremely cautious. Brian is a small, stringy man with eyes very dark and soul-less. When he talked to me, his head would tilt slightly to one side, and he had a smile that would not leave his face. His hollow black eyes did not blink, and he appeared to stare right through me. All I could think and feel was how creepy he looked, but since my mom said she loved him, I wanted to give him the benefit of doubt. It felt really good to see my mom again, and I tried to push the years of not hearing from her aside and just be happy that she was back in my life. After spending a few hours with Brian and Wanda, we said our goodbyes and left.

Heather and I had made it in our relationship for over a couple of years now, but I caught her in some lies and finally broke off our relationship. She did not take the news well and begged me to stay with her. I failed to listen to her pleas, and moved on.

I was tired of getting money from illegal sources and decided a job would be in order. I put an application of employment in at a fast food restaurant a few miles from my home. A couple of days later, I was called in for an interview, and soon I was an Artic Circle employee. I was not there long before I met Terri. She worked the front counter, and I was on stationed at the grill, but we could not keep our eyes off each other. I turned on the best charm I had to offer, and she was soon smitten with me. Through our conversations, I discovered that she was engaged to be married, and guess what? Her fiancée was on a mission for the Mormon Church and was far away (does this sound familiar?). Terri had a car, and she offered me rides home. The first time she drove me home, I thanked her for the ride, and she drove away. We talked later about that ride home, and she said, "If you would've asked me inside, you could've had me right then."

Well, it was not long after that we did start having each other, wherever and whenever we could. From the storage room and bathroom at our work, to the many parks around town. We went at it like rabbits. Terri knew I was not a good Mormon boy, but she didn't care. We both gave each other some desperately needed attention and fell in love.

Ted's girlfriend, Donna had talked him into getting rid of Natasha. I came home one day, and found out Natasha was gone. Rushing into things must have been bred into me, and on a whim, I took it into my own hands to replace her. Without any notice to my father, I came home with a German Shepard, and a day later Ted gave me an ultimatum.

"Get rid of the dog or get out," he said. That same day I moved into an apartment with a friend. "It was better this way," I thought.

The apartment was closer to my job, and it was much closer to Terri. It was in a run-down four-plex with three of the other apartments vacant. The people I moved in with did not last there long. I discovered after moving in with them that they were behind on their rent. I was only there about a week when they had to move out. The owner of the apartments knew that I was employed, and since I was the only one there, he offered me lower rent if I would manage the place for him. I accepted. **Now, I was eighteen, with a "day-job" and the manager of a small apartment building.**

"Boy did I have my shit together," I figured.

Just above Centerville are some mountains that were a great place for my friends and me to hang out and drink. One time, I brought my new dog and let him run around while we partied. His name was Shep, and he was only six months old. As we sat around talking and drinking our beer, Shep started barking, so we went to investigate. Shep was barking at a two-foot rattlesnake.

"Wow, I finally get to see a rattlesnake," I recklessly thought.

The snake was doing everything it could to get away from us, but I could not let it be. It started to slither into some rocks, and I grabbed its tail. It was fed up with me by then and turned to strike me. The snake's fang nicked the middle finger of my right hand and drew blood. That's when I should have had enough of the creature and let it be, but *not me*. I grabbed at the snake again, and it turned with its full-force sinking both fangs into my middle finger on my left hand (do not try this at home). The pain was intense, and I felt like somebody smashed my finger with a brick. I didn't panic right away; instead I grabbed the snake again. However, this time I caved his head in with a rock. "I just wanted to play with you snake, now look what you made me do," I painfully justified. With the snake dead, I got another rock that I used as an improvised knife and cut off his rattle. I wanted a souvenir.

By then, the realization of the snake biting me had set into my alcohol-soaked brain. "I'm going to die, I'm going to die," I began chanting. With me leading the way, we all ran down the mountain in a panic. We chanced upon an irrigation worker for the City who was working on one of the small water dams there. "I need your help. I was bit by a rattlesnake, and I'm going to die," I quickly explained to him.

"Where were you bit?" he asked me.

I showed him my left hand with the stream of blood oozing from the wound. I thought the guy would "freak out", but he had seen a snake bite before.

"The poison is going to my heart, and I'm going to die," I nervously reminded him.

"Calm down son, the poison's not even close to your heart," he calmly said. He took my injured hand, and he taught me how to tell where the poison was by the swelling in my finger. "You've still got a little while, but we need to get you to the Hospital," he explained to me. I felt great relief as I jumped into his truck. He drove me about five miles to Lakeview Hospital, and he rushed me inside the Emergency Room.

By the time I arrived at the emergency room, I was fairly calm and back to my funny, old self (I thought). I often used my solid wit to get me through very bad times, and this time was no exception. I was laying on the bed with my hand soaking in an unknown solution, and the pain pills I was given were taking affect on my brain. I began to crack jokes and have a good time with the bad situation. The Doctors around me had not dealt with a snakebite injury before, and they appeared stressed. I cannot recall exactly what I was saying, but one of the Doctors turned to me and told me to, "Shut up."

"You need to be quiet, so I can figure out what we need to do," he sharply said.

"Sorry dude," I calmly said to him, then zipped my lip.

The University of Utah Hospital was well equipped to handle my injury, so that's where I needed to go. After a twenty-minute ambulance ride, I was delivered to the Critical Care Unit of the Hospital. The swelling had reached above my wrist, and an IV was inserted into my arm with anti-venom trickling in.

By now, I was supposed to be at work, but it was looking like I was going to be a *few days* late. I used a phone to call work and break the bad news to my boss.

"Theresa, I was bit by a rattlesnake, so I won't be in today," I casually told her.

There was a short pause, and then Theresa spoke back, "Quit bull-shitting me Derrick, we need you today."

I reassured her I was telling the truth by handing the phone to a nurse. The nurse was happy to explain my stupidity to my boss.

I ended up spending three days in the CCU, until the anti-venom took full affect and broke down the poison in my body. At the entrance wound on my finger, the venom destroyed a small portion of tissue, which left me with a permanent reminder about playing with rattlesnakes. When I got out of the Hospital, I settled back into my apartment. I went back to work with a great story to tell about my battle with the vicious beast, and I loved the attention it gave me.

Shortly after my return, Terri informed me she was heading to New Jersey to work as a Nanny. I really loved Terri, so I did not take the news very well. I was beyond slicing my arms with razor blades or thoughts of removing my fingers with hatchets, but I was still not sure how to cope. Terri gave her notice at her job, and I began to completely ignore her. This upset her and she confronted me about it before she left. We expressed how we felt about each other and said we would write back and forth. She wrote me a couple of times, but I never replied. We went our separate ways, and I forgot about her.

After my eighteenth birthday, I received news from my lawyer. Three years after we began the lawsuit from our burns at Bauer, I was given 30,000 dollars. Well, it was that amount on paper, but after my lawyer was paid, I ended up with only eighteen large in the bank. (Don't you just love Lawyers?)

"Hum," an eighteen year old with eighteen thousand dollars, this could be either very fun, or very sad.

CHAPTER SEVEN:
A DOGS LIFE

With my miniature windfall and Terri gone, Artic Circle could keep me no longer. I quit my job, and began looking for the "baddest" muscle car I could get my hands on. Through a friend, I found a 1970 Dodge Challenger R/T, and it was mine for 2,200 dollars. The car had a 383 big block engine, four speed manual transmission, beautiful metallic brown paint job, and no brakes.

The same night I brought the car home, some friends and I "tied one on" and decided, brakes or no brakes we would take it for a drive. As I backed out of the driveway and applied the brakes, the car did not stop. I killed one of the apartment's mailboxes and put a long scratch in the beautiful paint of the Challenger. It was only a minor setback for us, and after I cried over the scratched paint, we all jumped back in the car and sped off. The first road we took was up hill, so slowing down from the 75 MPH we reached was pretty easy. I made a right turn at the top of the street, pointed the car down hill, and hit the gas. Now, with gravity and horsepower working for us, the car rocketed down the hill. Our speed was close to 100 MPH, when I noticed a stop light up ahead. I released the accelerator and started pumping the brake pedal; trying to squeeze whatever stopping power I could into the car. The car slowed a little, but not enough to keep us from barreling into the intersection. After doing a complete circle, the car came to rest in the middle of the road. Luckily, it was later at night, and the intersection was clear of other cars and people. I looked around in the car, and everybody inside was giving me the, "lets not do that again" look, but I slowly drove the car home. That is when I learned brakes are an important feature on a vehicle, so the next day, my car was in the shop getting a complete brake job, new rims, and new tires. By the time I was finished, I dumped over 6,000 dollars into it.

The car was not the only thing I put my money into, I was a generous partier, and soon there were many people at my apartment, partying the nights away. At one of my many parties, I met a girl named Wendy, who took a fancy to me. As quick as I was in the sack with her, I was in a relationship with her. Sex was either a tool for me, or a hindrance. I wasn't sure which. Wendy was not a particularly beautiful girl or my type, but because she was giving up the "booty", I automatically felt obligated to her. I also had a new roommate. We discovered through this small world of ours, we both shared the same foster parents. It just so happened that, when I hastily moved from the foster home, he was the one that took my place. Through our commonality, Brandon and I became good friends. He expressed to me that he would like a pet. Soon after, I chanced upon a small white kitten so I took it home, and gave it to him. I had my girlfriend, my dog Shep, and responsibilities I did not care to address. Brandon had a much more level head than I did. He was working, paying his bills, and taking care of his new little feline friend.

My girlfriend lived about fifteen miles north of me, and often I would drop whatever I was doing to go see her. I left my dog and other responsibilities with Brandon, and I drove my car to her house. Wendy was from a broken home, as I was. Her mother was a divorcee, and she appeared to be starved for male companionship. Wendy lived with her younger sister, her mother, and her grandmother. They lived in trash and dog filth, but from the beginning of my visit there, her family treated me like one of their own. They had a large back yard that was filled with undernourished Afghan Hounds, living in run-down kennels. In the basement of their house, was a dog grooming shop where they tried to make money. By the looks of their surroundings, they did not appear to be doing well financially. Wendy's mother made "passes at me" all of the time, and sometimes even with Wendy nearby. Wendy didn't seem to mind the attention her mother was showing me, but I did. I became uncomfortable with her mom staring me down, or "talking dirty" every time we saw each other. I confronted my girlfriend on her mother's behavior, and she just "blew it off".

"She's just playing around," Wendy would tell me.

I was three years older than Wendy, and I knew if I chose to pursue her mother's advances, she would have "gone all the way". I stayed there a full week once, and I'd finally had enough of the filth, both physically and mentally. I had to get out of there. After my unpleasant experience in that house, I could no longer look at Wendy the same way ("booty" or no "booty"), so I broke up with her.

I went back to my apartment, and when I arrived there, Brandon had some bad news for me. Apparently, while he was at work one day, my dog treated his kitten like a chew toy and killed it. Brandon was, understandably, upset with me for leaving so long. He explained to me that he was devastated when he went home and found his pet in four separate pieces. He "booted" Shep out in the street, and a car hit Shep. His back was broken, but Shep managed to crawl home on his front legs, and then he was picked up by animal control; who put him to sleep. Brandon and I both felt bad about what happened to our animals. We said heart-felt apologies to one another, and tried to move past it. We each understood our responsibility in the death of our pets. I think that made it easier to remain friends. If this had happened earlier in my life, the results could have been different. Although, I do not consider myself a violent person, I might have kicked his ass for killing my dog. **We both grew-up a little that day, but I still had a long way to go.**

The only direction I seemed to have in life; came from my peers telling me where to get drugs or alcohol. I cannot recall any of my friends "flipping the bill" for the stuff, and after a short three months of this wild lifestyle, my eighteen grand was down to about 3,000. I was not paying my rent, and my landlord started looking for me. I stopped answering the door when he came by, and I could hear him cursing me out on the other side. My money was almost gone, along with any shred of "good luck" I might have had.

The money I had left was spent on the things I wanted to spend it on, and skiing was one of those things. After a day of skiing, I came home and drank the last beer in the refrigerator. The call was put out to get more beer, so I got in my car and headed to a small store that I knew I could buy beer at. There was a nice Asian man that owned the store, and he never bothered to check my ID. Coming back from the store, the roads were slightly damp from a light rain. I turned the corner on the road leading to my apartment, and I mashed the accelerator to the floor. The tires broke loose and a cloud of white smoke barreled out of the back of my vehicle. I was having a good time with it until I noticed red and blue lights faintly coming through the smoke screen.

A police officer lived right by my apartment, and he was just arriving home as I was laying my smoke screen. I pulled the car over in the driveway; he jumped out of his car, and ran over to mine. The officer put his hand on one of my tires. The tire was still sticky from the intense friction that I had subjected it to, and I was "busted". The officer immediately said, something to the fact, that I must be pretty stupid to do that by his house. I could not argue with him, and I apologized for my stupid behavior. It was too late for apologies. And after a few minutes of the officer checking my information, I was in trouble. I did not have a driver's license thanks to the hit-and-run I had earlier in my life, and apparently I forgot to register my vehicle with the great state of Utah. Oh yeah, I did not have any insurance either. The nice policeman gave me a choice; they tow the car or I go to jail. I made my choice, and the car was taken away to the impound lot.

I was upset that my car temporarily belonged to the police, so I went to the Courthouse to find out what was required for me to get her back. I was told that I needed, the same things that I would have needed for my car to keep from going to "car jail", proof of insurance and registration. Because of my hit-and-run, I was supposed to have an SR-22 insurance policy. I had to pay a lot of money for that policy, plus another 100 dollars for the registration. When all of that was taken care of, I got my car back. However, I still could not drive until my license was re-instated. I parked the car and placed a "for sale" sign in the window. The asking price was 3,000 dollars and worth every penny. A lot of people looked at it, but nobody had that much money, so it sat on the road.

While my car collected dust, I continued to party the days away. In between my celebrations and avoiding my landlord, I met another girl. She was a pretty blonde named Karen. Of course, as quick as my penis was inside her, I was madly in love. Karen lived in, my old town, of Sandy, and without transportation, it was difficult for me to see her. I knew my time in the apartment was coming to a close, so I decided to find a place to live closer to Karen. I looked in the newspaper, and I found a mobile home for sale. It was located a few miles from her home. The price was right along with the location, so one of my friends drove me over to look at it, and it looked like shit. The trailer was a complete mess, but that did not stop me from spending my last 3,000 dollars on it. I was accustomed to making stupid decisions, and this purchase was no exception. I moved in with no money and no job in the middle of an exceptionally cold winter. When the heat was turned on in my crappy home, the trailer thawed, and the, now, un-frozen pipes below it, sprang several leaks. I didn't have any money to pay the plumber, so the car I loved and put thousands of dollars into was sold to a car lot for 1,200 dollars. I paid 800 bucks to the plumber, and I planned to live off the remaining money as long as I could.

It did not last long. Soon all my money was gone. I was penny-less and starving for food, my survival instincts kicked in, and my mind began searching for a solution. I was hungry, people, and my empty stomach begged for food. (Cat lovers; please stop reading through the next few paragraphs.)

My large gun collection that I cherished had been pawned away piece by piece. Only one gun managed to make it this far with me; a .22 caliber rifle.

My new neighbor's had several cats, and one of them liked to "hang out" in my yard. Hunger, plus feline, plus gun, equaled a meal for me. Every time I heard the cat meow, my empty belly told me to eat it. My thoughts were two fold; silence the cat, and fill my stomach. With every "meow," a mental picture formed in my head of the cat roasting in my oven. On my third morning without anything to eat, I loaded the rifle and waited for the call. Like clock work, the cat's call seeped through my walls. I looked out the window to assess the situation, and I determined it was time to get breakfast. It was early in the morning, the streets were clear, and the cat was thirty feet from my door. I cracked the door open, aimed the rifle, and with a small "POP" the cat fell dead. I instantly felt horrible, and ran out to get the dead feline. I brought it inside and looked at it for several minutes debating what to do next. I killed many times before this for a meal, but never had I harmed anyone's pet to cure my hunger. I was alone, I was hungry, and I cried for the life I had just taken. Though I'm not sure if it were for myself or for the cat, but I concluded not to put the cat through any more torment, so I put him in a plastic bag and carried him to the side of my home. Using the same pan I was going to cook him in, I dug the best hole I possibly could in the frozen ground. Then I apologized to the fallen creature and buried him.

I went for over a week living on Top Ramen; that I was able to buy from scraping my change together, and during that week, I went out and found a job. I started working at a Pizza Hut within walking distance from my home, and I acquired a dead-beat roommate, from my old friend Matt. His job was shoplifting, and he did that well. The guy would go into a store by our house, steal small amounts of high-dollar items, and then return them for cash. He never made much doing this, and we needed more. I thought growing marijuana could be a good source of income, so I used my first paycheck to buy some growing paraphernalia. I replaced the overhead light in one of the bedrooms with a small halogen light; then I filled a planter with soil, and put a few choice seeds below the soil. I certainly knew how to smoke marijuana, but I had no clue how to grow it. After a couple of weeks, the little seeds sprang to life, but they died three days later. I left the lifeless sprouts where they lay and forgot all about them.

I was depressed and felt quite alone. On Valentines Day, my girlfriend ditched my "sorry ass" and went out with someone else. I was at the end of my rope, and I decided suicide would bring me some much-needed relief. I took my rifle, loaded it, and put the barrel square between my eyes. I then touched my finger on the trigger and tried to prepare for my end. I sat on my bed for several minutes wondering if the small bullet would kill me right away, and I started to get nervous. My sister's husband, Steve told me a story about a friend of his that tried to commit suicide, in the same fashion that I was attempting. From what Steve told me, the bullet entered his friend's skull and looped around the outside of his brain. It did not kill him, but instead, severally handicapped him. I remembered the story, and I was scared it might happen to me. I went back and forth in my mind about where I was, where I had come from, and where I was going. Plus, I was terrified of becoming a vegetable, since there was no one to care for me.

The final thought of, "where I was going", along with my fear of the "dark-unknown" helped with my decision, and the choice to live won the battle that was taking place in my mind. I pulled the rifle from my head, removed the bullet from the chamber, fell back on my bed, and wept like a baby over what I had subjected myself to.

The next day my girlfriend came over and attempted to show she cared for me. I was still pretty torn up about the situation I was in the night before, and I freaked out on her.

"It was Valentine's Day, where were you?" I asked explosively.

I was not physically violent to women, but I did have, "the look to kill" that was hereditarily passed onto me from my father.

"I was this close to killing myself," I said, gesturing with my fingers.

By then, I realized I was freaking her out so I calmed down. We apologized to each other, and for some reason she stayed with me for a short while, anyway.

I still had several friends who liked to party, so party we did. The good times were less frequent now, but when they happened, they were full force. A drunken bash was planned for the evening, and people were invited to sleep over if they needed to. The morning of the event, some friends and I wanted to play football at a park. It was February of 1988, and we could not have asked for a better day. The Sun was shining, and the temperature was well in the 60's. After arriving at the park, teams were chosen, and our football game started. Back in those days, we didn't play touch football, tackling was the only thing allowed. My team got the ball first, and since I was the athletic type, the ball kept getting thrown to me. About six plays into the game, I had already touched the ball at least five times. The other team quickly figured out the biggest threat on my team, and they were out for my blood. The next play, the quarterback dumped a short pass off to me. As soon as the ball was in my hands, I was swarmed by at least eight people. I carried the pile, until the weight of everyone caused me to fall down. One or more players rolled onto my leg, and I heard a loud, "SNAP!" When the pile of people, finally got off of me, I looked at my right leg. The bottom half of my leg, just below my knee, and my entire foot was pointed up toward my face.

"That doesn't look right," I said observantly.

I fell back and screamed for somebody to get me, "HELP!" The pain in my leg was unbearable, and I started going into shock. I kept a level head by not looking at my mangled leg, and I tried to relax. Ten minutes later, a rescue crew arrived and rushed me to, an old-familiar place, The University of Utah Hospital. I had a compound fracture with my Tibia broke in two places, and one break in my Fibula.

I was in the Hospital with a broken leg, but my roommate decided to go on with the party plans. I was not there to keep the good time manageable, and the next morning I awoke in my hospital bed, to some Police Officers in my room. They told me about the great party I missed, and how they had to "bust it", and then they gave me some bad news.

"We found "pot" in the bottom of one of your friend's sleeping bags," the officer told me.

"Okay, that's not so bad," I thought.

"We also found a room for growing marijuana at your house. Can you explain that?" he asked, kindly.

I found myself in a very well known position, and I didn't want to lie to them. I explained how I was searching for other means of income, and that growing marijuana seemed to be the winner out of them all, at the time. The officers thanked me for my candor and said they would, "get back to me."

On the evening of my second day in the Hospital, the friendly Civil Servants appeared at my bed again.

"Good news Derrick. Because of your current situation, and the fact that the plants we found were small and dead, no charges will be filed," one Officer explained.

"Cool this truth thing was becoming useful," I thought. I apologized to them for my infraction and said, "It won't happen again."

They left, and I felt a great deal of relief. The last thing I needed was trouble with the law. I was eighteen now, and I did not want any jail time, especially with a broken leg.

When I left the Hospital I went to stay at Karen's home. Her parents were devout Mormons, and they did not approve of me sleeping with their daughter. Karen must have been able to communicate with her parents about our sexual activities. It was very uncomfortable for me to stay there, but I had nowhere else to go. I was on a hide-a-bed in their living room, and her father came in to "grill me" on my sexual prowess.

"How many women have you had sex with?" he asked me.

"Three, including your daughter," I lied.

Karen's dad sat next to me, with hopes to intimidate me, but I am not easily intimidated, so I laid back and conversed with him. This guy was clueless, and he kept prodding me for information.

"What's so great about sleeping with other women, don't all vaginas feel the same?" he ignorantly asked.

With that question, he succeeded in his quest, and all of a sudden, I was intimidated. I could not have felt more uncomfortable at that moment. I was lying in their living room with no mobility, wanting to run for my life.

"Is he really this stupid, or just completely sheltered from the real World?" I confusingly wondered.

When his questioning ended, Karen wanted to know what we talked about. I relayed the "meat" of our conversation, and she did not find it odd at all. I wasn't there long, before I wanted to get out. They freaked my mind, and I was very apprehensive staying there. I needed a place to go, so in a last ditch-effort, I called my mom and asked for help.

"Mom, I need to move in with you," I explained to her.

Wanda thought she could make a try at being my mom again, and she invited me into her home. I would guess Brian and Wanda had been married about a year by now, and when I first moved in with these people, things seemed normal. They rented a house in downtown Salt Lake City. I moved into a room across the hall from my mom and Brian. I felt like I had a family again. My last several years were rocky and it showed, so it was nice to feel some stability again. All I wanted to do was recover from my injury, and heal the ill feelings I had toward my mother. I was grateful to her for accepting me back in her life, but there was still animosity bottled-up inside me.

Due to the severity of the breaks in my leg, I underwent an operation that placed a 14" steel rod in my Tibia. I needed the operation or my right leg was going to be about a centimeter shorter then my left leg. My mom showed me love, and she did a lot to help me through the surgery and recovery. Brian acted kind toward me also, and initially, we all got along well. I settled into their home and focused on my healing.

One day the doorbell rang, and I hobbled on my crutches to answer it. A Sheriff was at the door; what a surprise, he was looking for me. He served me with a subpoena from the trailer park I had just moved from. When I moved in with my mom, I gave my run-down trailer to my run-down roommate. I gave it to him because I no longer wanted to deal with it. The home was in very bad shape, and I just wanted to wash my hands of the "giant head ache". I knew that the few months we lived together in the trailer, he never paid me a dime, so there was no shock to me when he didn't pay the lot fee and got "booted out". The trailer was still in my name, so they came after me. I ended up signing the home away to the owner of the trailer park, and they finally left me alone.

My baby sister, LouRee was living with Brian and Wanda before I moved in, and it was nice to have her living there, although, LouRee was not home much because Wanda made her work. At twelve years old, my sister had a job at a movie theater and was making a whole two dollars an hour. Wanda never gave her a ride to or from work. She had to walk the mile and a half (one way), even after she got off work at night. LouRee was working for Wanda, and every payday she signed over her forty-dollar paycheck to good ole' mommy. Our mom would tell LouRee how strapped for cash she was, but that didn't stop Wanda from buying a brand new Pentax camera. Wanda had been into 35mm photography for several years by then, and she had aspirations of becoming a professional photographer. Her new camera was *top of the line*, and she told me she spent over 1,200 dollars for it. After Wanda got her new toy, she gave me her old Olympus 35mm camera, in hopes that I would follow her lead in photography. I did not follow her lead; instead, the camera was lost to a Pawn Shop not long after she gave it to me.

Karen was coming to see me at times, and for some weeks after my move we did all right as a couple. Even though, we had sex during her visits, I could tell our relationship was coming to a close. We were not comfortable with each other anymore, and Brian did not want us alone in my room together. She was young and had more mobility than me. Karen used her freedom to find someone else, and she broke up with me. I was a little upset, but knew we were done.

I had some support in my life now, so the transition from Karen was not as bad as it could have been. Brian and Wanda did their part to comfort me on the split, and I was thankful to them.

At this point Brian and I got along smashingly because of a similar interest. My early rock lifting and football days guided me to the hobby of weightlifting. Brian was more into cardiovascular and toning exercises, but our hobbies were along the same path. The things he seemed to enjoy the most were, "eating for health" type of books. He always talked about them, and he showed them to me whenever I appeared interested. Brian would talk about how certain foods could cure certain diseases and was very adamant about it. I didn't necessarily disagree with Brian; I just usually took a more pessimistic approach to things. Most of our conversations were about exercise and diet, but sometimes I liked to "give him hell" on his choice of religion. From what I knew then, Wanda met Brian in her Church ward house. I don't remember who gave me this information, but they conveniently left out the fact that my mother met him in a Church drug-rehab program.

By now, my friends, you have read that I used many drugs in my days. Nothing too serious, but I definitely used acid on more than one occasion. I looked at many of my friends, and even myself, on drugs at the parties I attended. I began to suspect that Brian was "whacked-out" on acid or a similar substance. I found it entertaining to see Brian come home with his pupils the size of basketballs, and pretend he was sober. He could have fooled my mom, but he certainly was not fooling me. It was in these states that Brian's brain seemed like translucent goo, and I would carry on, somewhat, philosophical conversations with him.

"What made you chose the Mormon Religion?" I asked him.

"What do you mean?" he answered back.

"I mean, with so many Christian-based religions; what brought you to the Mormons?" I clarified.

Brian is a "die hard" Mormon, and I wanted to learn what convinced him to join that particular religion. He told me a story of how destitute his life was at a certain point, and that he had no direction.

"Okay," I thought. "Those are the usual suspects in one's transformation." "What's wrong with Jehovah Witnesses or Catholics? Why can't you be something instead of a Mormon?" I asked.

Brian told me a story of how, like his buddy Joseph Smith, he was searching for answers to the "one" true religion. Brian went about it slightly different than his buddy, Joe, from the idiotic fable he told me. After ingesting twelve hits of some quality acid, he traveled through the desert and spoke to God, a small donkey, and the anus of a Gila monster (the last two he did not speak of. I am just trying to make a point of how ridiculous I found this). Our conversation ended that night when I basically told him; anyone taking that much acid, would most likely talk to God, or a cactus if they felt so inclined. That was the point he knew I was on to his "bullshit", and he started disliking me.

My friend, Matt from Centerville was still hanging out with me. He invited me out-of-town for "Spring break," and since I wanted to get out of the house for a while, I agreed to go. I was still using crutches, but was mobile enough to get around. Matt drove us over 300 miles, south to the city of St George, Utah. We had a great time there, and I did pretty well on my crutches for being intoxicated. After a four-day party, we made it home. When I got back, Brian and Wanda were different people, and they now acted strange. In my short absence, they went from the shallow side of the pool, straight into the deep end. Brian fed LouRee's pet rabbit to her, disguised as a B-B-Q chicken dinner while I was gone. And he stopped letting her watch regular television. She could only watch KBYU, a Mormon operated public television station. I started developing a bad taste for Brain's actions, and I went back to my original way of feeling that Wanda was a little "off her rocker" for falling in love with this clown.

I was there almost a year, when the discovery was made; we were not going to like each other for much longer. My leg was almost healed, and I was now living in their basement, but I was still jobless. Our similar interest was no longer relevant because I realized Brian was "not right", and I got the feeling Brian no longer wanted me living there because he had no control over me.

The last day I was at their house, I was in my room minding my own business when Wanda came in lecturing me on going to Church and following her and Brian's wishes of a "wholesome Mormon family". I don't know if Brian said something to Wanda, or if she came down on her own accord. My guess is, from the knowledge that I have since acquired; Brian was probably tugging at her strings. I remember it was 8:00 pm, and I was on my bed relaxing for the evening. Wanda came in and sat on my bed and *in my space*. I did not feel like dealing with her bullshit. I just wanted her to leave me alone.

"Can we talk about this tomorrow, mom," I calmly begged her. She did not take my hint and kept pressing the issue.

"I worry about you Derrick, I'm worried you're going to hell," she cruelly said.

I'm sure Wanda knew what she was doing. She kept pushing my buttons. My mom wanted me to, "blow-up" because that would give her reason to kick me out of her house.

"Mom, I don't need this right now. Would you please leave me alone," I pleaded, as my voice level rose.

"I love you Derrick, I'm not leaving until you hear me out," she continued.

That was the point of no return for me. I exploded with, almost, all the rage of my father. (I say almost because I did not hit her.) I did find something to hit, however, and I jumped up and destroyed my stereo, as I screamed at her to leave me alone. That stupid bitch played me, and I fell right into it. Now the stereo I cared so deeply for was gone.

"Oh see - Derrick, I'm terrified for you. You're just like Ted," she cried.

I was not quite sure who I was, but my father I was not. That was it for Wanda and me. Our relationship would never be the same. I called Ted and asked him if I could move in with him. He agreed to let me move in. I knew this would be a risky venture with my dad because of what he did to my brother Richard. While Richard was living in Ted's condominium, my dad re-married. He had already shipped LouRee off to live with Wanda, but my brother remained there. Richard had a job and was not a dead-beat, and frankly, my dad was an asshole and wanted time alone with his new wife. Without Richard knowing what was going on, Ted sold the condo, and he and Donna moved out. My brother came home from work, one day, to an empty house except for a "dear son" letter.

Ted and his new wife Donna were now living in a mobile home in North Salt Lake. Since I had the approval from my father, and I had moving down to a fine science, I was soon out of Brian and Wanda's disillusioned lives.

CHAPTER EIGHT: WOLF PACK MINE

I moved into Ted and Donna's house physically and mentally wiped out. I could have easily sunk further in life, but I decided to see if I could pull myself to a new level. With some encouragement from my dad, I got my G.E.D, passing the test with flying colors.

I found a job, through my friend Matt, building out-door lights. I was finally developing a life for myself, and I was finally learning some responsibilities. At nineteen, life was kind to me, and my dad was too. It seemed Ted could never stay in one place very long, and after living with him for only a couple of months, my dad was ready to move. Donna and Ted bought a house, and Ted offered to sell me his mobile home. I jumped at the opportunity to buy the home and did so for 150 dollars a month, plus the lot fee. I finally had my own home again.

My job was okay, but my boss was an idiot. I cannot remember the exact situation that brought me, wanting to kick his ass, but I avoided it and decided to quit instead. I knew my dad would be upset when he found out that I quit, so I had to find something fast. Soon, I was frequenting the local military recruiting center. I was talking to members of all branches of the military. Ted served in the Navy reserves, and he talked to me about joining for their educational benefits. I needed a High School Diploma to get the job I wanted, but I was two-and-a-half credits short of my diploma, so I signed up for a Social Studies class at Granite High School, and two short months later, I had my Diploma.

The Navy hounded me to join their elite group, and I decided to go to Fort Douglas, in Salt Lake City, to take the ASVAB test. The test was designed to determine an individual's skills so the military could decide if you should be a cook or a jet fighter. I fell somewhere in-between, so I had several jobs to choose from. Richard and I took the test for the military at the same time, and he and I were always very competitive. Richard did better with the ASVAB than me, but I did better with the little blonde that happened to be testing with us. In between testing and our physicals, Richard and I commented on our mutual liking of this young woman. While we moved from room to room together, Richard began a conversation with her by telling her how "hot" she was, and I think he even grabbed her ass. After that, I knew it was my time to shine, so I started conversing with her. It did not take long for my charm to woo her, and soon I had a date with a pretty young lady, named Jennifer.

Jen and I had a lot in common, she was one year younger than me, and we were both going into the Navy. She lived north of me, over twenty miles away. I didn't have a car, but that was not going to stop me from seeing her. We began dating and spending every minute we could together. I was a very fit twenty-year old man by now, so I easily rode my bike the twenty miles, one way, to see her.

She worked at a dry cleaner's shop, and she was usually there by herself. I used those opportunities to see her, and in-between her dry cleaning duties, we were all over each other. Jen was a virgin when we met, and I thought it was time to change that. A week into our relationship, she came to my house and spent some time with me. Jen gave me her virginity, so I quickly gave her my love.

After the test for the military, and only a short time after Jen and I began dating, I changed my mind about the Navy. Jen did sign-up with them, however, and she was scheduled to leave for Boot Camp soon. Because of our newly found love, the two of us did not want to be apart. Jen and I talked about getting married when she got out of the Navy, but I was afraid with her gone for two years, we would not make it.

One day, I was riding somewhere with Ted, and I relayed Jen and my conversation about wanting to get married, but not wanting to be separated. The first words out of my father's mouth were, "Why wait?"

"We just started dating," I reminded him.

"Well if you're going to get married one day, you might as well make it now," he said.

I questioned him on why we should so soon, and he explained to me how our military benefits would be much greater if Jen and I were "hitched".

"Okay, he had me convinced," I thought. "Now if I could just convince Jen."

Ted let me borrow his vehicle and with swiftness, I was at Jen's work holding a dozen roses. She was surprised to see me, but the real surprise was yet to come. I handed her the flowers and asked for her hand in marriage.

"Are you serious?" she asked with a shocked look on her face.

I told her I was very serious, and I explained to her about my conversation with my dad, and it made sense to Jen, so three weeks into our relationship, Jen and I were man and wife; thanks to 30 bucks and a Justice of the Peace.

Shortly after the ceremony, Jen decided she did not want to be in the Navy, and we went together to tell her recruiter. A small fuss was made, but Jen reminded him that she could just get pregnant, and he left us alone.

My earlier concerns about relying on my father soon surfaced. Ted came to me and told be he was selling the trailer that Jen and I were living in. His actions did not surprise me, but I was upset with him. Jen and I were freshly married, so Ted offered to let us live in his home. Ted and Donna had a large house in the Salt Lake valley, and there was plenty of room. Without anywhere for us to immediately go, we moved into their home and started our life together.

Not a month after we were married, Jen and I were in the bathroom checking the color of a pregnancy test.

"What color is it?" I impatiently asked.

"Give it another minute," Jen said.

Less than a minute later, I looked at the stick and saw the blue on it; that meant baby. We were both excited, but my excitement quickly changed to fear when I realized I didn't have a job. I went back to the military recruiter for help, and soon, I had my right hand raised for the US Army. The recruiter tried to talk me into driving a tank, but I wanted nothing to do with that profession. I compromised on the duties of a Heavy Wheel Vehicle Mechanic, and I got the GI Bill and Army College Fund thrown in also.

I had about five months of freedom before leaving for Basic Training. So I tried to make the best of it, by blowing shit up. When I would get bored during the day, somehow, pipe bomb supplies made their way into my hands. After unpacking a box at our new home, I found a container of black powder from my muzzle-loading days. I recalled my earlier scout years, and I wanted to see if I still had my talent for destruction. I found some fence pipe and cut three pieces, 8" long, and drilled a small hole in the center of each. After crimping one end, I filled the pipes half way with the gunpowder, and I closed the other ends of them. I inserted a fuse in the center of each hole, and in about an hour, three improvised pipe bombs were in my hands.

My dad's house was next to a busy road, and there was a large brick wall separating the two. The house was on a corner that came off the main road and entered into the neighborhood. In the front of the house, the wall was only two feet high, but as it wrapped around the corner, it graduated to six feet. I figured this would be the best place to test my homemade WMD's, Weapons of Minor Destruction. I took the first one, and I buried it six inches into the ground, lit the fuse, and stepped back. The ends of the casings were not crimped tight enough, so when the fire hit the powder, the energy escaped without much happening. I went back to the "drawing board", and I took a hammer to the crimped ends, smashing them tightly closed. (Again, do not try this at home, or anywhere else for that matter.) I took the second one, and placed it in the hole that I'd dug out for the first one. I waited until there were no cars in either direction and lit the fuse. I stood about twenty feet away, watching the fuse disappear. As the fuse faded from my sight, I caught a glimpse of a car coming from the corner of my eye. The timing of the approaching car synchronized with the fuse and, "BOOM!" I saw the shock wave skirt over the two-foot brick wall, and smack the passing car. The explosion scared the shit out of both of us, and he swerved into the other lane, as I ran away. I turned to see if anyone was chasing me, and they were not. I dumped the last bomb in a neighbor's garbage can, ran inside our house, and hid in the closet for a couple of hours. I was home alone, and I sat there hoping I would not hear a knock on the door. The knock never happened, and through a little luck, I did not wind up in a Federal Prison.

In May of 1990, I was shipped off to Fort Jackson, South Carolina, to learn how to be a soldier. I easily fit into my new role, and I had something in my life, that before I had not; "discipline." I thrived off the knowledge the military paid me to learn, and I excelled at it. I was very motivated to be a soldier, and one time in the chow line that motivation cost me. In Basic we were instructed to say our last name and the last four numbers of our social security number, as loud as we could, to the Drill Sergeant doing head count. Four weeks into my training, I screamed with too much enthusiasm, and "blew-out" one of my, now governmentally owned, testicles. I went through a hernia operation at the Post Hospital, and then I was shipped home for three weeks of convalescing.

I had no idea on what *normal* families needed, and I was selfish like my mother. In my marriage, I came first. I thank this to the examples taught by my parents. It was near my twenty first birthday, and I convinced my wife to buy me a 600-dollar present. The gift I wanted was a, stupid radio-controlled truck, and the cost was not an issue for me, but Jen had a problem with it. My birthday present cost almost our entire savings at the time. She was thinking of our future child, and I was only thinking of myself. She did give in and buy me the gift I wanted.

My few weeks on military leave quickly came to an end, and I was back in the great state of South Carolina. The people I had started Basic with were only a week away from graduation. So, I was recycled into a unit that was at the same level I was at when I left.

Soon after I was back, I easily made the squad leader of my platoon. Everything the Army threw at me, I accomplished and did well the last four weeks of my training.

During Basic Training, Jen and I wrote love letters back and forth all the time. By the time of my graduation, I wanted to see her real bad. She wanted to see me too, but she didn't want to fly, being six months pregnant, and she also did not want to spend the money on a plane ticket. I wasn't concerned about any of that, as long as my needs were taken care of. She flew to Fort Jackson to see me graduate Basic Training, and we spent a few days together.

After eight weeks of learning the proper ways to kill a man, I moved to the next level of military training. Advance Individual Training or, AIT as it's likely called. Some soldiers go to different Posts, but I stayed at Fort Jackson. My job in the Army was to be a mechanic of their largest wheeled vehicles. I had some experience taking apart stolen bicycles, but that was the extent of my mechanical knowledge. However, I understood that with a little effort on my part, learning the job would be easy. I was given more responsibility at the Barracks now. I moved up from Squad Leader, and I was now a Platoon Guide. A Platoon Guide is responsible for his entire platoon.

I was a leader all my life; except before, I led people the wrong way. Now I had big responsibilities, and I was in charge of over thirty fellow soldiers. As I look back on this, I realize it was a major turning point in my life. Even though I still had a long way to go, a solid foundation was finally being built for my integrity.

After twelve weeks of mechanic school, I passed with flying colors. I received a special ceremony, on top of the regular graduation, and I received a diploma with HONOR GRADUATE printed on it. It was a big accomplishment for me, since only one award was given per company (there were over 400 people in my company alone).

Two weeks before I went home, Jen did one of the best things in the World. She gave birth to our son, Andrew. She was an absolute champ with the whole pregnancy thing, and Andrew's birth was no exception. Three hours after Jen entered the Hospital at Hill Air Force Base, we had a little five-pound four-ounce baby boy. The two weeks I had to wait to see my son, seemed to take forever, but when I got off the airplane and held him, time stood still. I knew my son would be loved, but I was terrified for him.

"Would I be like my dad? Would my son be like me?" I had several questions and doubts battling in my mind when I held my son for the first time, but a final thought came through and silenced the others. My son was quiet and sleeping when I first held him, but I saw something that broke me down, and made me weep tears of relief. **My son gave me a feeling that I had not felt for the twenty-one years of my life; "hope", and it overwhelmed me.**

I was not my father, nor was he I. Andrew was my son, and as far as I was concerned, he would not go through what I went through in my life. Sure, I knew we had a long road ahead of us, and my parenting skills were almost as bad as Ted and Wanda's. I still knew in some way, on some level, I would do better than my parents did. It was a great feeling to think this. Now, if I could just make it happen.

I was only home for two weeks, and then I had to ship off to my duty station at Schofield Barracks, Hawaii. I used the short time home to try and reconnect with my mother. I called her up, and asked her if she wanted to meet her new grandson. She seemed pleased by my news, so Jen and I jumped in the car with our little boy and headed to my mom's home. After driving over 25 miles to get there, we knocked on the door, and nobody answered. Jen and I commented on how strange it was that they would not be home. After all, I had just talked to Wanda, and she should have been expecting me. As we scratched our heads, Wanda peeked out of the window blinds. She was purposely ignoring us, and it was very upsetting. Jen was confused by Wanda's behavior, and I don't know what part Brian played in my mom's decision not to let us in their home, but I thought the whole incident was par for the course, and we left.

Shortly after that, I was shipped off to Hawaii, putting Brian and Wanda in the back of my mind. I was in Hawaii a whole month, before Jen and Andrew finally made it with me, in Paradise. A run-down duplex, a mile from my duty station, is where we initially made our residence. We paid 750 dollars a month to live there with several hundred cockroaches, but it was "Hawaii," so we learned to live with them.

The ground war of Desert Storm was beginning at this time, so the Army had me very busy. I was not home that often, and this left my wife and son to create a strong bond together without me. Jen was a great mother, and it showed. She spent every minute she could with Andrew, and she did everything for him. I did nothing, but bring home some money and spend it on myself. I made sure they had the basics; food, clothing, etc., but after those needs were taken care of, it was all about me. I was spending money like crazy. I was buying engine parts for my new pastime (building race cars), and financing my old pastime of radio-controlled cars. Jen was upset with my uncontrolled spending, but being the good wife she was, she hardly said anything. After one year of living in the duplex, we got orders to move into military housing. This was a two-bedroom town-home, owned by my "Uncle Sam". Thanks to the good ties I had with my Uncle, we lived rent-free. This finally gave us a chance to save some money and become a healthy family unit. (You know me well enough by now, to know I probably wasn't ready for that yet.)

Jen and I were married young, and I was still very immature. I'm sure that the promptness of our marriage was a factor as well, and after two short years of marriage, I started doubting the choice I made. I felt too young to be married, and I was in over my head. The lust I had for my wife faded, and so did my love for her. I made myself a victim to my family because I thought "they" were holding me back. I was now consumed by my own selfishness and it grew and grew. I was never physically abusive to Jen or Andrew, but my ignorance hurt us all.

My wife continued to love me, and she put up with all the waste I shoveled into our relationship. I started doing things to avoid my family altogether. I took advantage of Jen's dislike of the ocean. I bought the finest snorkeling gear and used it all the time. I was surrounded by water, and I felt free of my responsibilities. The more I "hung out" with my friends, the less I wanted to be with my family. **Playing "victim" was working well for me, just as I was taught growing up.**

Something was bound to give, and eventually it did. At home one evening, Jen confronted me on my sour attitude toward her. I played dumb for a while, but she knew better so she kept prodding me.

"Jen I want a divorce," I said calmly.

She was upset and immediately started crying. There were times before this that I'd mentioned divorce, but that was because we were arguing. This time was different, and Jen knew it. I was calm, collected, and focused on what I wanted to say. With that painful realization to Jen, I sank a knife into her heart. All the sacrifices she made for me, and all of the crap she had put up with, suddenly meant nothing.

"Well at least I know why you've been acting this way," she cried to me.

"I don't love you, and I'm not happy," I callously said.

Jen is a good lady, and she did not want to end our marriage, but I wanted out. I moved into the Barracks on Post, while Jen and Andrew stayed in the military housing.

I temporarily put my family behind me, and I enjoyed the separation. Jen continued to hang on to our relationship, and she waited patiently for me to come to my senses. She befriended a wife of a sergeant in my unit, and she was spending a lot of time at their house. It was not long, before I was at their home also, spending time with my family again. We had been separated about a month, and I missed Jen's intimacy. Jen understood what it would take to get me back. She threw out some bait, and I bit. One night I went to visit at Jen's friend's house, and my wife was looking great. At first, we didn't say much to each other, and then she said, "We need to talk." We went behind the house, and down to the river that ran nearby. Not much more was said by either of us, but soon we made love. After that, I was in love with my wife again.

Jen had her pathetic husband back. By now, we had been in Hawaii for over two and a half years, so our time in Paradise was coming to a close. Jen and Andrew went home to settle back into civilian life, and I stayed at the Barracks a couple more months to finish my active duty, before making the trip home. Jen lived at her parent's house, until a week before I got home, and then she and our son moved all our belongings back into Ted and Donna's home. After an emotional reunion at the airport, we were a family again. We didn't last very long at Ted's home because he was driving us nuts, so we wanted to move. I kept in contact with my friend, Greg over the years, and he informed me of a basement apartment for rent across from his home in Riverton, Utah. I had a swing shift job loading trucks with metal roofing, and Jen had a job during the day. We moved into the basement apartment for 300 dollars a month and functioned as a family.

Working swing shift gave me an opportunity to finally get to know my son, and we began to bond. My son and I were doing several things together, and I discovered Andrew did very well at the things he was interested in. At three years old, we bought him some roller blades, and soon he was teaching me how to use those contraptions. Every type of wheeled vehicle we could put under Andrew, we did, and he picked up on how to operate them real quick. I found myself doing something for my child that my parents never did for me. That was encouraging him to do things he enjoyed, and supporting his endeavors. **I learned my son could bring me a lot of happiness, and we became the best of friends.**

Sometimes when I encouraged Andrew, I reflected on my past and wished Ted and Wanda would have done that for me. It felt good to know Andrew was doing better than I did as a child, but it gave me a false sense of security. I was still completely selfish, and most of the money Jen and I brought in, was spent on stupid shit for me. Not realizing it at the time, I was testing Jen to see if she was the person I wanted to be with for the rest of my life. Jen took everything in stride, and this made me care less and less for her. Without my wife reciprocating the kind of distorted love I showed for her, I began to feel like she was not the right person for me again. Three years after our first separation I felt like our marriage wasn't going to last much longer. Of course, I was too chicken to communicate this with her, and I continued focusing on myself.

My friend Greg got a new truck so, naturally, I wanted one. Instead of a vehicle Jen could drive, I made sure the one I picked would be difficult for her to operate so she would not be able to use it. Jen showed great patience and continued to be a good wife. I had no means of coping with her wisdom, and I looked for a way out anywhere I could. My "out" finally came while I was watching my son one day. The phone rang, and upon answering it I heard a familiar voice from my past.

"Hi Derrick, this is Heather," the voice said.

"Hi Heather, it's been a while. What brings you to call?" I asked.

"I'm dying from cancer, and I only have a few months to live. I'm calling everybody to say goodbye," she somberly said.

I was shocked, and asked her if she was "serious". She reassured me she was, and I set up a time to meet her and talk before she left the earth. I did not tell Jen about the phone call, and that evening, Heather and I sat down at a local mall to talk.

Heather looked good for a person dying from cancer, and I was instantly attracted to her again. I do not remember our entire conversation, but when I told her I was not going to be married much longer, her cancer suddenly appeared to go into remission. I recall feeling uncomfortable about the remarkable recovery she seemed to experience in my presence, but I just chalked it up to my cancer ignorance. She went from terminal to remission in the few short hours since we talked on the phone. But I did not care, and the next day I told my honest and loyal wife; I was divorcing her. Jen was, once again, devastated as a result of my ignorance, but she *still* wanted to be my wife. Since what she wanted was never important to me, the next day she packed her belongings and went with Andrew to her parent's house.

Heather and I quickly became an item again and rushed into, what we thought was something meant to be. It wasn't long before we moved in together or talked about marriage. Neither of us had anything going for us, except for our own personal desires to "fuck our lives up" any way we could. Heather's mom, (my earlier step-mom) was now on her eighth husband, and that should have given me some clue. It did not, however, and I rolled with the punches.

For over a year Jen continued to maintain some kind of hope for us, but she eventually came to my work with divorce papers. By now, I was feeling pretty stupid about my decision to leave her, but it was too late. Jen was over me enough to move on, and so she did. I signed the divorce papers, and I signed full custody of Andrew over to her as well.

I guess I was back in a relationship I needed; one filled with lies, drama, and all the bullshit-love I, so deserved. Heather continued with her story about making a full recovery from cancer, and I began to question her. She originally told me she had an ovarian cyst, or something like that, but I also recall her saying she had lymphatic cancer as well. I did not know if she was going up, down, left or right, and it started to bother me. I confronted her on what I felt were lies, and that pissed her off. In return, I would get upset, because she thought I was stupid enough to believe her. Yes, I did a lot of stupid things, but a moron I was not.

Jen and Heather did not like each other; as I am sure you could guess. This caused me to lose touch with the miracle that brought me so much hope originally, my wonderful son, Andrew. I was consumed by Heather's torment, and I was not going to let anyone ruin our sick love. I had to live with Heather, and Jen was no longer my wife. In some perverse way, I tallied this circumstance up to Andrew no longer being my son, and I figured I would be better off with the two of them out of my life. Jen came after me for child support, and I did not want to give her a dime. Right before our divorce, we filed chapter13 bankruptcy, I was making the 425-dollar a month payment to the trustee, so I could still drive that stupid truck. I complained to Jen with no relief, and the only thing I could think of was giving up parental rights to Andrew. That would have got Jen and Heather off of each other's back, and it would have got me out of paying to support my son. I was in a bad place in the World, without the knowledge that I was the one doing it to myself. Ignorance is bliss, but my stupidity was causing me a lot of pain.

Jen talked to her lawyer about me giving up rights to Andrew, and he informed her that there would have to be another male figure in his life for me to do that. Jen was not married, and she did not plan on getting married any time soon. (I dodged a bullet that time.) I cannot imagine what life would be like without my son, and I am grateful it did not go that far. Heather began to accept Andrew as my son, and for a short while we all got along okay.

I have always been an avid camper, and I thought it would be nice for Andrew to go with Heather and I so we could spend some time together, bonding. It was typical for me to take firearms when I went camping, and a semi-automatic .22 went with us this time. Andrew was barley five years old, and I carelessly thought he was old enough to use the weapon. After setting up camp I loaded the gun, and shot it rapidly at a row of cans. I loaded it again, and handed the weapon to my son. Heather was sitting on the tailgate of my truck, and I was standing to the side of Andrew. He had no problem pulling the trigger, and he wanted to fire it rapidly like he saw me do. Andrew swung the weapon in a circle away from me, and continued firing as the barrel headed towards Heather. Three shots were fired before I could pull the gun from Andrew's hands, and two of the bullets barely missed Heather. I was scared from the near miss, and I sternly told Andrew to never do that again. Andrew started crying, and that was when I realized it was my ignorance that almost caused a tragedy. I consoled my son and told him the accident was not his fault, and then I apologized to Heather. Andrew and my relationship became stronger from the incident, but Heather's and mine did not.

Our relationship was the typical rollercoaster type I needed, but eventually it began to wear on me. Shortly after our camping trip, I broke up with Heather. I left her at our apartment high and dry. I moved back with Ted and Donna, but I was there less than a month when Heather convinced me to stay with her again. She found another apartment for us, and I was back with the "queen of lies." I paid every bill we had together, plus my child support, and bankruptcy payment. Heather worked, but all of her money was for her. When I was broke and in need of some gas money, she would bitch about it, and reluctantly, "lend" me twenty dollars. **What comes around goes around, and I was finally getting mine.**

Heather's objective in winning me back became clear one day. I came home from work, and she was gone. She accomplished what she wanted, and that was to end our wicked relationship on her terms, and not mine. Her leaving mentally wiped me out, and I became severally depressed. I was wondering why I was even on this messed-up planet and if I was ever meant to succeed at anything.

CHAPTER NINE:
TICKS AND FLEAS

My mother was not in my life now, and it had been at least seven years at this point since I spoke with her. I completely lost touch from her, and she lost touch with the World. During my military service, Brian and Wanda decided to get rid of their belongings, and to live off the earth and preach "Brian's brand of Holy Crap". Brian gave up his good paying job at O.C. Tanner, as one of their jewelry designers, and Wanda quit whatever job she had, so she could follow a freak.

This was the first story I heard about the two, and it did not make any sense to me. In the first stage of their homelessness, I figured, Brian made the decision to avoid Uncle Sam. I remember conversations with Brian that included him thinking everyone paid too many taxes, so I assumed he talked Wanda into disappearing in the lives of hobos, to avoid paying taxes.

Initially, Brian built a handcart, and they loaded it with the bare essentials to get them by. They took off across the country to New York; they were on their own mission to teach about God and, supposedly, the Mormon faith. They managed to survive by panhandling, and Wanda played piano for money. Their mission took them over a year to accomplish, and then they were back in Utah, and they started living in the mountains. In the warm months they slept in a tee-pee, and during the winter they stayed at Brian's mother's house. They were off the map, but firmly embedded into the Utah geography. It became fun for my family members to talk at gatherings about Brian and Wanda. It was like a game of "Where's Waldo", except replace Waldo with Wanda and that was what our conversations consisted of.

Brian and Wanda panhandled for their money, and they did very well for themselves. They put on an act that they were poor, but always shopped at the most expensive health food stores. People would see Brian begging for money at one corner, and then walk a few paces to a "Wild Oats" store, to buy quality food. Brian was absolutely full of shit, and my mom fell for every bit of it. My brother Richard had dinner with the two of them at our grandmother's house. During dinner, Richard asked Wanda if she was on drugs, and her response was an, unconvincing "no." Richard basically told her that if she was happy and doing what she wanted, he would support her. I did not feel this way, however, and thought what they were doing was quite stupid.

Brian seemed to have my mother in his complete control, and it was clear to me that part of his controlling her, was to keep my mother from talking to her kids. I was not happy with Wanda by now, and I certainly was not happy with Brian. At this point, I thought he was severely disturbed and my mother severely affected. With every story I heard about them, I could imagine my fist connecting with Brian's head and popping it like a grape, but I never laid a hand on him; instead I took comfort in my vivid imagination and left Brian alone.

After Heather dumped me, I moved to Woods Cross, just a few miles north of Salt Lake City. I still had a good job, and a friend at work set me up with a room in a bachelor pad. Another company bought the company I worked for and they were now expanding. I had worked for the company for nearly four years, and I was the shift supervisor when the company was sold. They wanted to put me in a salary position, and they began training me for such. During my employment, I made several friends that worked under me. The new company was training me to be an asshole to the people I already had established a rapport with. I was conflicted in my decision to keep a good job or keep good friends. I decided to keep the friends and lose the job, so without any notice I walked away.

There was a Movie Buffs, video store just a few blocks from the dump I lived in so I went there often. I was passing my time away by watching Jackie Chan movies. My split from Heather was in its fifth month, and I thought I was ready to try the dating game again. There was a young lady who worked the video counter at Movie Buffs that I started taking a fancy to. I was not thinking of any long-term relationship plans, I just wanted to try my hand at dating again. I brought her lunch on one occasion, and before I could say, "Be kind rewind" I had a movie date at her house. Our date started normal enough; we talked for a while getting to know each other, and then we began watching the movie. Pretty good, huh? Yeah, that's what I thought, until her doorbell rang and her boyfriend was standing there.

"Okay, he could be a cousin or a brother," I cautiously thought.

When he sat down in the chair next to mine, his status became clear. The girl I went there to see sat on his lap. I did not say a word. I pondered the predicament I was in, and after sitting there for ten uncomfortable minutes; I had enough and got up to leave. The next day, I went to the video store to get some answers and was hit with one of the biggest lies I'd ever heard.

Sara also worked at Movie Buffs. She was a tall and beautiful brunette, and I never talked to her before. The girl I had dated the night before was not talking to me. I figured it was her loss, and I rented a movie. I almost made it to my vehicle, when Sara intercepted me and gave me some shocking information. I cannot remember that psycho's name (the girl I dated), but Sara told me what she said when she came into work that day. Apparently, the psycho told Sara that when I was at her house the night before, I kicked her ass and blackened her eyes because her boyfriend showed up. Wow, that was just a little too close to home for me. I may have been a selfish prick, but I had never physically abused any woman.

"I hope you don't think that's true," I told Sara.

She said she didn't, and told me she'd caught that girl in several lies. I thanked Sara for the information, and went back in the store to confront the weirdo. She was at the far wall restocking movies when I approached her.

"Why did you say all that about me?" I calmly asked. "I was nothing but kind to you, and now I come here, and get hit with this," I continued.

She could not even lift her head up to talk to me when I confronted her. She softly apologized to me, and I left the store. Sara was still outside. She was just getting off work and ready to leave. I thanked her for the information, and she invited me to go smoke a joint with her. I had quit smoking weed thanks to the military, but I did not want to pass up the opportunity to talk to Sara. She laughed at my jokes while I drooled over her beauty. I thought she and I made a perfect match, so I asked her out. Our relationship quickly bloomed, and we began to see each other exclusively. Sara was only nineteen years old, and I had over eight years on her, but because I typically rushed into things without thinking, our age difference did not seem to matter.

Immediately into our relationship, the red flags were there. I should have turned and ran away as fast as I could, but *not me*. One evening Sara and I were talking, and she told me that she was a bi-sexual vampire. She said she was reluctant to tell me this because she was fearful Vampires were going to kill her. She was not afraid of my reaction to the "bi-sexual issue. The Vampire issue did not bother me all that much; it was the bi-sexual comment that got to me because of my insecurities. This conversation took place only a couple weeks into our relationship, and I already had thoughts of marring her, so I wanted reassurance that she was not going to leave me for a woman later on. I learned that Sara's bi-sexual experience was from experimenting with her best friend, and one of their boyfriends. They had a threesome one time, and that was it. When Sara told me the story, I scoffed at her and tried to put it into perspective.

"That doesn't make you bi-sexual; it makes you bi-curious," I said with a chuckle.

My comment pissed her off, and she angrily stormed out the door. Sara got into her car and left for a few minutes, then came back. I figured she would break up with me right there, but unfortunately it did not happen. We quickly made up, and her actions proved to me she would be the one to make my life miserable, and since misery loves company, I fell head over heels.

I got a job at a construction company. The job did not pay much at first, but Sara was still working too, so we discussed moving in together. We had only been dating for a month, but we found an apartment and moved in together. Our engagement was the next step. The lumps from my past were still fresh in my mind, and I had learned something from them. I didn't want to rush into another marriage, so I set our engagement to last a year.

Sara is the youngest in her family. She had two older sisters and an older brother. Sara's oldest sister was already married, but her other two siblings were not. One of her other sisters, Kathy, was experiencing young love at the same time Sara and I were. She already had a date to be married and it was scheduled before Sara's date to marry me. This bothered Sara because she and her sister were very competitive.

When I got home from work one day, Sara surprised me with some news about our wedding. She informed me that our wedding had to be moved eight months ahead of schedule to ease the stress on her parents. "Why doesn't Kathy move hers up?" I asked. "We could keep our date the same, and see if your sister would change hers," I reasoned with her.

Sara wanted to beat her sister to the punch, and she was not going to take "no" for an answer from me. I was cautious that she might be too young for marriage, but she easily talked me into it. I was trapped, I didn't want to lose her, but doubts had already formed in my head, and I was unclear if Sara loved me. She reassured me that I was the one for her, and our wedding date was planned for September of that year; which was eight months earlier than I originally hoped.

Sara came from a successful upper middle-class home, and I worried the lifestyle she was accustomed to would be out of reach for me. I communicated these feelings with her, and she assured me it didn't matter to her, and she convinced me her love for me and my son was genuine. Although she was only nineteen, she really took a liking to my son, and this made me very grateful. Sara did a lot with Andrew and me, which was a big selling point to me. She was a drastic change from my recent Heather days, and I found our relationship refreshing.

Our wedding was in her parents' back yard, and Andrew was the little ring bearer. He was a tender six years old and looked great in his tuxedo. Andrew performed his job well, and the ceremony went off without a hitch. Our reception was also a hit. We had many people there. Sara had a Polynesian band play, complete with fire dancers. It was a good time for everyone, and a prelude to what I thought would be a wonderful life with her.

At twenty-seven, my life was going well again. I had a desire to do better for myself and find something to succeed at. I sat down and wrote my goals on paper, both short term and long term. The short-term goal was simple; find something I liked to do and learn it. The long-term goal was also simple, I figured; become a success by the time I was thirty-five years old, which at that time I imagined would be through financial gain. I communicated my aspirations to Sara, and she seemed willing to support my endeavors.

Our relationship started off very well. Sara's parents, Edward and Penny, were kind to me. They showed more love and support to me than I'd ever experienced from anyone. It was not just her parents. Sara's entire family genuinely cared about me. They were always commenting on my ability to make them laugh, and they enjoyed my drawings that I shared with them. A short time before meeting Sara, I started drawing pictures of cartoon aliens in an attempt to explore my creative side. With my new family's support, the, "Naked Aliens" were born, and I felt like there was a reason to live. I loved seeing their reactions to the misadventures I put the aliens through, and it fueled my desire even more. I was not sure if the comics would succeed, but finally I had some direction. To this day, I love Sara's family for the support they gave me.

Sara was a different story though, and she appeared annoyed with what I was doing. Her happiness seemed to come from her ability to control me, and I think she worried that my success would have diminished her control over me.

My insecurities started rearing their ugly heads, and our union began falling apart. A few months into our marriage, Sara got a job in the mailroom at a large company. I did not mind her working there, until one day she came home talking about a male friend she'd made at work. It bothered me because; I knew what my objective was when I befriended women. Sure, I was projecting my own feelings into the situation, but still I felt there was some validity to it. Sara did not want to validate anything I was saying and became irritated with my insecurities.

I was getting what I lacked from my first marriage, conflict. Sara's personality was the type that ran away from issues until she could deal with them. Mine was the type that hated to feel abandoned, and I would have rather settled things on the spot. This was definitely not working for us and only six months into our marriage, Sara moved back home.

I remember the day clearly. We sat on the couch to watch television. I felt great sitting by my wife, and I was gently caressing her chest, just above her heart. The "Simpson's" were on, so I was laughing and enjoying myself. I noticed Sara was not making a peep, and she should have been laughing at that episode.

I questioned her, lovingly. "Is something wrong, sweetheart?"

Sara then pulled away from me with a sobering look on her face. With that, I instantly knew what she wanted to say. Before she could say it, I let her off the hook. "You're sorry we got married, and you want out." I said, clairvoyantly.

"I'm too young for this Derrick, and I can't take it anymore," Sara spoke back.

Like a lot of young women, Sara thought marriage would be similar to the "fairy tales" she'd learned as a little girl. She did not realize the work and commitment involved. I had somewhat of an understanding, thanks to my first marriage and my eight years on the earth longer than her. I was upset with Sara, but without much of a fuss, I let her go. Once she was gone, however, I wanted nothing more than to remain her husband. I would call her relentlessly, pathetically begging her to stay with me. My pleas to stay with Sara did not work, so I stopped calling her.

I developed a "wild hair", which influenced me to purchase a used sports car. It was funny how Sara wanted nothing to do with me, until she saw my car. The next thing I knew she wanted to be my wife again, and I moved into her parents' house with her. Sara and I were together again, but our problems were far from over. She convinced me all of the problems in our relationship were because of me, and she remained in full power. We were working at being a couple again, and I devoted most of my attention to Sara. I was at a point in my life where I wanted nothing else, except to be close to my wife and make our marriage work. I had already been through one divorce, so I was determined to stay married. I did not understand it at the time, but the "Karma Police" were poised to treat me like I was Rodney King. It was my turn to feel how my first wife must have felt in our marriage.

I still had a constant in my life, my son Andrew. On a weekend after having him over, the three of us got in the car to take him home. Andrew was now a very bright, eight-years old, and he had never met his grandma, Wanda. It was by coincidence that Brian Mitchell's mother lived by Jen and Andrew, and I spotted them walking on the side of the road that evening.

"Hey Andrew, do you want to meet your grandmother?" I asked him.

"Sure, dad!" Andrew said excitingly.

Wanda and Brian were on the opposite side of the road, heading for the Home Depot down the road. (I remember this confused me because they did not have a home.) I whipped the car around and headed into the parking lot, and then I pulled up along side of my haggard-looking mom.

"Hi Wanda, it's me," I said.

The two completely ignored me and continued walking. "Okay maybe she did not hear me," I confusingly thought.

I stopped the car, got out and walked toward them. "Wanda, it's me, your son, DERRICK!" I sternly reminded her.

Those two *buttheads* kept walking, so I walked around them and got in their faces. "Don't you want to meet your grandson?" I begged her. Brian and Wanda did not say a word and walked past me. I got back in the car and consoled my son.

"Is that my grandma?" Andrew, unknowingly, asked.

"No it's not Andrew, don't even worry about it," I said angrily.

Sara didn't take Wanda's cold shoulder too well, and she asked me to pull up to them. When I did, she rolled down her window and gave Wanda a "piece of her mind".

"How fucking dare you!" Sara said with complete confidence. "You bring six children into this world, and you can't acknowledge their existence," she, bold-fully, spoke.

They, of course, continued to ignore us and moved along. Sara wanted to follow the two freaks into the store and continue verbally lashing out at them, but I decided against it, and we left them alone.

I was sure Brian, now had total control over my mother, and she could no longer speak to us. They had been on the streets for at least five years. He had my mom on a watermelon and lettuce diet, and that must have starved Wanda's brain of some much-needed protein. I think this diet helped him to have total control over my mother, and she seemed very content with the way things were. I always knew Brian disliked me the most out of Wanda's children because I never approved of his extremist lifestyle. I often made jokes at their expense, plus he knew I could see right through him. Resentment was mutually shared between Brian and me, and I imagine if it were anyone else in my family that approached her that night, Wanda would have been able to talk with them. If I did not have Sara and the comfort of her family at that time, I probably would have lashed out at the two, and maybe I would have beat Brian into a bloody pulp. **I was very content with my new family and that helped make Brian and Wanda's stupidity easier for me to handle.**

Sara's Parents enjoyed getting their family together, whenever and wherever they could. Penny and Edward loved to travel, and Sara and I often went with them. Monterey, California, was one of our favorite destinations. I enjoyed taking those vacations with my beautiful wife, for the most part, but there were times Sara would "act out" and make it miserable for me. Our relationship was filled with several ups and downs, and vacations were no exception. Sara and I could make love for many hours on a secluded beach, and then fight viciously over something stupid. Without knowing it, I had a wife that helped me be comfortable in my own misery. Blindly, I put myself in that kind of relationship. I was familiar with it, and although I was receiving pleasure from pain, I loved every minute of it.

After living at Edward and Penny's home for a couple of months, Sara decided it would be in our best interest to purchase a home. The truck I selfishly purchased in my first marriage had been repossessed. I changed my original Chapter 13 bankruptcy to a Chapter 7 and wiped out my debt. My credit was crap, and Sara's had not been established yet, so getting a loan for a home was going to be difficult for us. Sara started looking for seller financing, or rent-to-own houses, and her searches led her to some pretty bad neighborhoods. She was frustrated, and she got upset with me when I told her to have some patience. After she threw a tantrum, I caught her looking in the paper for an apartment. The new dwelling was, now going to be just for her, and it pissed me off. I confronted her new decision and she told me, "If you're not willing to move, I'm going to leave."

"What the hell, are you going to leave me here?" I asked her.

"I don't want to live in my parent's home forever," she bitched.

I found myself in a situation I knew all too well, and I recalled how my mother would act when she wanted something. Sara was acting just like my mom did, and I fell for it. Her behavior was helping me realize what I was consumed by this woman; I just did not know how to get out. After all the drama, we settled on a house in Kearns, Utah, and we moved into the seller-financed rambler. Our house was a "fixer-upper", but it was not in as bad of shape as our marriage.

One evening at home, my night started out very well. I'd spent the week before this working at my day job then working on my alien drawings afterward. Sara had conveyed to me earlier in the day, she wanted to spend sometime together because she felt like I was neglecting her. I agreed and told Sara when I got home from work that evening the night would be ours.

After I arrived home from work, my brother, Richard called me and asked how things were going. I told him I made a couple more cartoons that I would show him when I went to his house to drop off a DVD I borrowed from him. Richard only lived a couple miles from my home, so I hurried over to run the small errand. I got to my brother's house, dropped off the video, grabbed a beer, showed him my cartoons, and made it back home in less than an hour. ("Danger, Will Robinson, Danger.")

"What the fuck were you doing at your brother's for so long?" Sara screamed at me, as I walked through the door.

"I dropped off a video and showed him my latest cartoon," I said confused.

Permanently adding her name to the rest of the psychos in my life, she said something I will never forget. "You want to butt-fuck your brother," she screamed at me.

Wow, that was a new one for me. I could not believe what I'd just heard. I tried to ignore the horrible comment and reason with her.

"Sweetheart, I was gone less than an hour. It's only 6:00, we still have plenty of time to do something." I logically said.

She did not want to listen to reasoning and continued to assault me (and other members of my family) with her foul words. I am the kind of person whom will try to reason at first, but once I've reached my limit, I can shred people with words of truth. I grew tired of the mouth-bashings from her, and escalated the incident to a new level with my words. The truth, I spoke worked, and Sara jumped up to kick me out of the house.

"Get the fuck out," she told me.

Well, my friends, enough was enough by now, and I was tired of being the one that had to leave every time we argued. Sara was pushing me out of our bedroom door when I decided she should be the one to leave this time. I turned around and grabbed her, pushing her into the hall.

"You get the fuck out, for a change!" I forcefully said.

I closed the door, and Sara freaked out more, "I'm calling the police! You're not going to get away with abusing me," she boasted.

I panicked because I knew I would be the one to get "screwed" by the law, but Sara had already dialed 911. I was not going to be around to get arrested, so I took off. I drove around for a short while, then parked the car and waited. When I felt enough time had passed for the chaos to die down, I went home and tried to patch things up. I was wasting good Spackle, though because the hole I was trying to patch was beyond repair, nonetheless, I patched away.

Sara was content on creating my grief, and she began causing turmoil between my ex-wife and I. Jen and Andrew moved to San Diego because Jen had remarried, and her new husband's job required them to move. Sara talked me into seeing a lawyer to find out if I had to pay for the entire trip for Andrew to come and visit me. The lawyer told me that Jen should pay for half of the cost, and Jen was not happy with that. I think, for the most part, Sara was trying to look out for the welfare of Andrew and me, but Sara successfully used their move as fuel to start a fire between Jen and me, and we all began to fight. I wanted to see my son more, but I did not want to hassle anyone over the issue. I went along with my present wife, in order to keep some level of continuity at home, but that was really causing more problems. Jen, her husband, and I wrote nasty e-mails back and forth, while Sara sat back and enjoyed the show. Andrew was caught in the middle, and I felt horrible. After a couple of weeks and some mean exchanges with words, we calmed down. We managed to heal most of the wounds, and Sara was upset that I made peace with them.

A year after moving into the rambler, our house payment went from 800 dollars a month to well over 1200 dollars a month. The home my wife wanted so badly was killing us financially, and our relationship was just as broke.

My wife was a *freak*. In the same sentence I heard, "I love you and I'm happy", she also said, "I'm cheating on you with my friend from work." Sara floored me with that information, but I still tried to hang on.

"I love you, Sara, and I forgive you." I said, with a crushed heart.

Sara could not believe I forgave her and thanked me for loving her so much. Her love for me only lasted another week, and then she came home and told me, "I want a divorce."

I was not surprised by the news, but I was hurt. I moved into Richard's apartment, depressed and feeling like a complete failure. The last thing I wanted was to be divorced again, and I could not shake it from my head.

I passed the time away sleeping and watching television, while darkness surrounded me.

CHAPTER TEN:
THE SHEDDING

I realize now that the darkness I lived in then came from years of festering waste I had subjected myself to. Unknowingly, my own ignorance engulfed me. My life always had its ups and downs, but this time I was extremely down. With Sara wanting nothing more to do with me, and my son over 800 miles away, I was at the lowest point in my life. Richard was annoyed with me because I was in his space, and because I went back to Sara whenever she would let me.

I would say, by now, she had evicted me from our relationship at least four times. I was older and thought wisdom came with age, but wiser, I was not. Like clockwork or a disease, Sara would come around and all it took was one look from her, and I was under her spell. At first, we kept our reunions secret, but eventually members of my family found out. They were understandably upset with me because they didn't want me to get back with her again. I wanted to be with Sara, but she felt it necessary to give me conditions. One: Find my own apartment and move from my brother's house. The next demand would end up being her downfall. Two: Go to counseling and change my behavior (since everything wrong in "our" marriage was "my" fault). Until these demands were met, we would remain separated.

Although this upset me, I wanted to end my darkness, so I searched for something I could do for myself. While watching television, I saw an advertisement for a computer animation school, and I had a thought to take my "Naked Aliens" from paper to computer. The next day I was at the school signing up for my college experience. I realized by now I had the ability to do the things I liked well, but I never knew how to pursue my talents. I was still trapped by Sara, and ignorant to the co-dependent life I lived, but something inside of me wanted to do better.

I soon started counseling sessions, and I learned the pain and torment that filled my life was brought on by me. "Creature of habit" was a phrase attached to my actions, and it brought my behavior to light. The lame excuse of being a "victim" was no longer going to work. I would now have to take ownership of my mistakes and try to learn from them. The counselor I was seeing prepared me to say "no" to Sara when she came to my door again.

"What are you going to do if she shows up at your door?" my therapist asked.

"I won't let her inside," I proudly said back.

"What if it's pouring rain outside?" she posed.

"I WILL NOT LET HER IN," I said with confidence.

I thought I was learning, until Sara came to my door and said, "We need to talk."

She'd found out I was starting school, and she wanted to be my wife again. All of the conditions she put forth, I completed. Now I was working on my future. This must have "ate her up inside" because she was losing control of me. She saw I was actually succeeding in life, and she couldn't allow that. By now, I was pretty sick of Sara, but I still did not want to be a twice-divorced man, so I warned her, this would be the last time I played her little game and invited her in. She was only inside my apartment for a couple of minutes when she told me she was supposed to be at a cabin with her boyfriend and his family.

"So, you're cheating on your boyfriend to be with your husband," I said observantly.

"No, I decided to be with you and break up with him," she argued.

Red flags popped in my head, but quickly went away after we made love for the first time in months. Whether it was a conscious action or a subconscious one on her part, Sara used her vagina as a tool, and I was madly in love with her once again. I moved into her apartment in downtown Salt Lake as soon as she asked me to.

I continued my Therapy, and School was a very important part of my life now, so I committed myself to it. When I started my college education, I still had a job, but thanks to the earlier choices I made when I joined the Army, I was now receiving 1,000 dollars a month from the "Army College Fund." The construction job I had was physically demanding, but I maintained it the entire time I knew Sara, so she understood I was tired of it. The company I worked for was not treating me well, and when I expressed this to Sara, she gave me the go-ahead to quit and focus on my schoolwork. I thought it was great that she would support me doing what I wanted, so one day took her up on it. While I was working on the freeway in 100-degree heat, I had enough and quit. I felt a great amount of love for my wife again, and for a short time we were doing all right. **I was excelling in school and making quality friends, instead of the loser type I'd made earlier in my life**.

I was feeling good about myself, and Sara did not like it when I felt good. It wasn't long before Sara became jealous of my school and my friends, and she started showing animosity toward both. Whatever I did, Sara did not seem happy with it. I followed the steps she laid out for me, but nothing was ever good enough for her. We argued over stupid shit again, and I wondered why I went back to this woman. I continued to focus my energy on school instead of on Sara, and I did my best to try and make Sara happy, as well as excel in my new endeavor.

Sara's mailroom job evolved into an Administrative Assistant. She loved this job because she got to travel at times. Due to my insecurities and abandonment issues, I was never thrilled about her new job. However, I decided to be a bigger man and put these feelings aside. With every subject or test I passed in school, a strong foundation of my own self-worth began emerging. Sara was right to worry about my success, because the more it happened, the less I needed her. This would not have been an issue if she supported me and remained true to our commitment. Even though she treated me poorly, I hoped she would grow out of it and she could remain my wife.

One morning, I put on my denim jacket to go outside, and I noticed a piece of paper in the pocket. Sara was in the shower when I found it, so I decided to call the number and see whose it was before jumping to conclusions. I called the number and let it ring. Nobody answered, but when the voicemail picked up, it was a male's voice and his name was Frank. I hung up the phone, went to the shower, and asked Sara, "Who's Frank?"

She instantly had that "oh crap" look on her face and knew she was in trouble.

"He's the guy I was seeing when we got back together," she explained.

"Okay, well since we're back together, why do you still have his number?" I asked.

"I ran into him at work, and I didn't get to explain why I left him," she said stumbling for an excuse.

I did not buy it and began packing my clothes.

"You're leaving me?" she tearfully asked.

"I'm not going to put up with this anymore, Sara," I angrily said.

While I packed some clothes, Sara cried for me to stay. At first her tears did nothing to persuade my decision, but after a few minutes, I calmed down and put away the clothes. Sara had the phone number to cheat on me again, and allowed myself to stay trapped. I let her treat me badly, because I did not want to be alone. Even the thought of her fucking someone else behind my back was better than solitude to me, so I kept my insecurities, and my wife.

Sara's brother, Bill found love, and he became engaged to the redheaded beauty he was smitten by. Her name was Jackie, and she was originally from Rigby, Idaho. After a short engagement the two of them planned a wedding in her hometown. Sara's Family along with she and I made the trip to Idaho to join in their union. During the reception, an announcement was made for somebody who was going to sing a song for the newlyweds. "Pete Barzee," was announced, and it floored me. I ran to Jackie's mom, who was accompanying him on the piano and asked her if I heard the name right. She confirmed it, and I told her I was from a line of Barzees. I was excited about the situation and confronted Jackie about it. During our conversation, I found out that Sara's brother Bill had just married one of my distant cousins.

"Was this a small World or what?" I happily thought.

I figured with this discovery, Sara would see that it was fate for us to be together, and she would love me more and treat me better. After spending the night in Idaho we came home and functioned as a couple, for a short while.

Sara went to Memphis, Tennessee, on a business trip. When she returned home, she was very excited and happy to see me. She had a surprise and wanted me to guess what it was. After a few clues, I concluded she got a tattoo. I was right, and she showed me the frog inked on her back with my name underneath it. My first thought of what Sara did was very stupid, however, I thought it was a big commitment for her to do that, and I thought she loved me more than ever. When I was younger, I used India ink and tattooed Heather's name with a heart on my upper left arm. With our demise, I scrubbed her name off my arm using a toothbrush and salt.

Sara proved to me that my original thought of the tattoo was correct before her *new* tattoo had even healed. I was home doing some schoolwork, and the phone rang. Sara was on the other end; she said she was calling from work.

I told her what I was doing, and finished the conversation by saying, "I would see her when she got home." I went back to doing my work, and less than a minute later Sara walked through the door. She was not at work, but using a friend's cell phone to call me.

"Hi honey," I gladly said. "I thought you were at work, what brings you home?" I asked.

"Derrick we need to talk," she quickly said.

"Oh shit this can't be good," I told her.

"I'm not happy, Derrick, and I don't want to go through this anymore," she explained.

That was the last straw Sara ever piled on my overburdened soul. Something was bound to give, and it was not going to be me this time.

"Oh well, we tried. I'll be out by the time you get home from work this evening," I calmly said back.

"Goddamn" that felt good to say, I finally had enough of her indecisiveness and those were the words I wanted to hear. Sara went back to work, and

I finished what I could of my project, packed a few things, and went to Richard's house.

Richard was pretty tired of my back and forth moves by now, and expressed discontent with my apparent lack of strength over this woman. I tried to reassure him that I was tired of the crap she piled on me for so long, but he did not really buy it. How could I blame him? During our short three-year marriage she had kicked me out so many times.

The wife I tried to love for so long was now a nuisance to me, and a barricade to my success. A second divorce was not an issue to me anymore, and I wanted that life-sucking parasite off my ass.

After about a month of living with my brother, he moved in with his girlfriend, and I was on my own. This time, alone was just what the doctor ordered. It helped me break away from Sara. I started to develop a lot of confidence in myself, and school became a great outlet for my creativity. Perfect Attendance, the Honor Roll, and the Dean's List became certificates I received after every quarter, in school. I took every assignment given, and I tried to out-better myself, as well as my peers.

"No way in hell was Sara ever going to have a man as good as me," I thought with a new confidence.

I liked the person that was emerging from the positive influences I subjected him to. I learned not to be a victim of my parents' circumstances any longer. Accepting ownership of my actions and their consequences, good or bad, was something "I" would have to do.

I still had to pass one more test, however, and that came with a knock on my door. I looked out the small glass panel when I heard the knock, so I already knew who it was. Through my many moves, and change-of-address forms, some of Sara's mail was coming to me. Two days before she came to my door, I took all of her mail and forwarded it. I knew the time was coming for her to show-up, and did not want to take any chances.

"Who is it?" I cautiously asked.

"It's me, Sara. I came to see if you had any of my mail," she said.

"I don't have any of your mail. I sent it to you a few days ago," I said through the closed door.

I heard Sara let out an, annoyed sigh because I would not open the door for her, and then she stomped away. I did it; "Hallelujah!" Sara's spell over me was finally broke, and she must have known it at that point, because she finally left me alone.

At school I had access to the Internet, so I took advantage of it and filed for a divorce from Sara on-line. We had no children; thanks to a miscarriage Sara had suffered on a trip from Idaho, so the transition was an easy one. I know that sounds harsh, but it was a good thing looking back. A child between us could have started another worthless cycle of abuse and pain for the people involved. I sent Sara divorce papers through the mail, she signed them, and I was free. In my mind, I wished her the best and hoped she would find happiness.

CHAPTER ELEVEN: FROM QUADRUPED TO BIPED

My grandfather, Gary passed away shortly after his 92nd birthday, and it saddened everyone who knew him. A large number of his friends and family showed up to bid him farewell at his funeral. The Thompson children, including myself, were talking beforehand about our mom and Brian. The conversation mostly consisted of whether or not they would dare show their faces, at the funeral. We all felt they would, so we remained alert for their entrance. Shortly into the service, the two robed *freaks* came in and sat down toward the back of the room.

LouRee was like every child that wants a mother, so when the two showed up at the funeral, she used the opportunity to try and get the answers she still searched for.

She wanted her question of, "Why aren't we good enough for you?" answered; and was not going to let Wanda off the hook, until she gave her an explanation.

After the service everyone followed the casket out the front doors of the chapel, while Wanda's kids were following her and Brian out the back. LouRee was hot on their tails and I was right behind her, when the two turned around and started screaming at us.

"REPENT, REPENT; CHILDREN OF ISRAEL, REPENT," Brian and Wanda bellowed at us inside the church.

"What the fuck are you talking about? You people are the ones that need to repent," I reminded the two dumb-asses.

They hadn't committed any crimes that I was aware of at this juncture, but I knew Brian and Wanda were far from being sin-free.

We made our way out of the church, with them still screaming at us. I remember thinking that I should just beat the shit out of him, but I decided against throttling Mitchell and instead made fun of him. As they yelled at the top of their lungs, a crowed gathered and watched the two make Asses of themselves. I used the opportunity to show Brian how stupid he looked, and threw my arms up and started shaking violently. "IT'S WORKING, IT'S WORKING; YOUR POWERS ARE WORKING," I hollered back, as they looked at me. I think that gave them an idea about how stupid they really looked. Brian and Wanda turned and walked away from us, going off the radar once more. My sister Rachel managed to snap a picture of them leaving, and after the incident, we all got a good laugh at their expense. Honestly, for me it was quite comical to see how distorted their reality had gotten. Although they made me laugh, I did not understand how serious it really was.

When I finished school I had new friends, and I felt like there was a world of options. I did not find a job in my new field right away, so I decided to take things into my own hands. I had an idea to take the 3D modeling skills I learned from school and apply them to writing and illustrating children's books. I began to do that, and I felt really good about the career I was making for myself. I finished a couple of the books, and felt great about my new life.

It had been about a year now, from when I saw Brian and Wanda at the funeral. They were out of my thoughts until one evening I turned on the television and watched "America's Most Wanted." I had not seen the program for quite a while, but that night I wanted to watch it. A few minutes into the program, a small segment was shown about my step-dad wanted for questioning in the Elizabeth Smart kidnapping. I freaked-out and immediately called their 800 number.

"I was just watching your program, and I saw my Step-dad profiled," I said with my heart pounding.

"Are you sure it was your Step-dad, and not just somebody who looked like him?" the person on the other line asked.

"I've known the guy for over fifteen years. Brian David Mitchell is my Step-dad," I repeated with confidence.

"We're going to want to talk to you," he said.

I gave them my information, hung-up the phone, and then tried to call the Salt Lake City police. It was in the evening and I could not get a hold of a detective, so I haste-fully called my brother, Richard.

"I just saw Brian profiled on America's Most Wanted, for questioning in the Elizabeth Smart case," I excitedly told him. Richard flipped-out, and the two of us just knew he had committed the crime.

"Richard, you realize that mom is going to have something to do with this also," I told him.

"Yeah, I know," he somberly said back.

Richard and I knew we had an obligation to our community to do whatever we could to help find them. We felt Brian was not a killer, but most likely a child-molester, so we hoped Elizabeth would be found alive, somewhere. We both figured we could find them pretty easy, so we set up a time that next day to look for them. We recounted the stories we heard about their "hang outs" downtown, and where we thought they might be, and then we looked for Brian and Wanda. Our search included the Greyhound Bus Station and some homeless shelters around the general area. From the people we talked to, we figured we'd missed them by a couple of weeks, but we kept looking where we could. Richard and I always disliked Mitchell, and I was looking forward to the opportunity to drag him by his beard to the police station. Richard had several pictures of Brian and Wanda; including some of him clean shaven, exactly what the media was looking for. Five months before he took Elizabeth from her home, Brian removed his beard because people were telling him he looked like Osama Bin-Laden. The non-scruffy Mitchell is whom the Smarts met, and we hadn't seen him in a while. We did not know if he still had his beard or not.

Richard went to our local, Fox 13 news with all the pictures he had. He did a story with them; and Rachel, Richard, LouRee and I went on "America's Most Wanted," and told where we thought they might be found. We had several pictures and knew they usually went south for the winter, so we told anybody who wanted to listen. Through the local and national media we felt pride in plastering Brian and Wanda's faces all over the country.

From the minute I saw Brian's profile on America's Most Wanted, I knew he committed the kidnapping. All the years that I had known Mitchell combined together at that moment, and I knew he was capable of the crime. It was a solemn relief to know Brian was the person I thought he was, and I wanted to see him brought to justice.

When the FBI and local police announced they just wanted Mitchell for questioning, members of my family began to have doubts that he kidnapped Elizabeth. The story was quickly dying down, but I stood firm and kept reminding everyone whom we were dealing with. I had a lifetime of putting myself, and other people around me through a lot of pain and suffering. Thanks to my personal choices over the last few years, I was lucky enough to have matured. **I understood it would take a lot to right the wrongs I made in my life, and I used this opportunity to start.**

After our interviews, the days turned to weeks and then into months. I could not believe the information we gave people did not have the two captured right away. I wanted them brought to justice, so I kept watching the local news for any information. Nothing happened for a few months, and I questioned Brian and Wanda's whereabouts.

"I wonder where they could be hiding?" I asked myself.

It was only a short ten minutes after thinking this question; I got a phone call I will never forget. LouRee was on the other end with the news we all waited to hear.

"Derrick, turn-on the news, the police just captured Brian and Wanda," she said with nervous excitement.

I hung up the phone, turned on the television and saw the news frenzy that was taking place. Sure enough, the two were captured as they tried to make their way back to Salt Lake City. Elizabeth was found alive and safe. Instantly, a series of emotion, from glad to sad ran through my mind. After all, I had a part in the arrest of my own mother.

The media got a hold of all family members that were affected by Brian and Wanda, and all of a sudden, our freaky parents' lives were exposed for the World to see. Which also meant, we as a family, were showcased for everyone to see. I found myself in unfamiliar territory; having to defend myself from my parents' actions and trying to prove I was nothing like them. It seemed like all of the work I did over the last few years were wasted, and I had to re-evaluate my life. People would easily judge me now because of my mother and stepfather. I felt like I was the only one who knew differently. I made incredible leaps in my personal evolution as a good man, and that now seemed to be ripped away from me.

All of the stupidity and bullshit I put myself through in life was now at the for-front of my thoughts, and although I do not condone Wanda's actions, I can sympathize for how she was trapped by Brian. Yes, she did it to herself and eventually she will have to take responsibility for that. I now know that she will not be able to do that until she stops playing the victim, and owns up to her actions.

It was not until I was about half way through writing this book; that I can say I completely understood the cycle I was in. In fact, it was through my writing, I finally began to understand who I was and why I went through that darkness in my life. Like my parents, **I was an animal, and it took a lot of pain and self-evaluation to stand up straight and walk away from it.**

I knew the phrase, "The apple doesn't fall far from the tree," but now, finally I had a clear concept of it, and I am able to "Spin Doctor" the phrase because I know; "Sometimes the apples get picked up, polished off, and sent to market, far away from the tree."

My younger brother and I visited Wanda in jail two weeks after her arrest, and it was one of the most surreal experiences of my life.

"What were you thinking mom?" My brother and I blurted out the question, at the same time, to her.

The smile she wore when we arrived quickly disappeared, and a stern look came over her face. "Chapter 7 Moroni, of the Book of Mormon," she said. Then, she began reading from the same. The handcuffs she wore gave just enough freedom for her to hold the small book and turn the pages. It was really quite a pathetic sight, and I almost felt sorry for her... almost. I do not know much about the "Book of Mormon," but what she read had to do with polygamy and taking on more wives.

I will not lie to you, there were definitely a few emotional moments with my mother, but that quickly turned into anger for me as she preached on. One minute she was my mother, the next she was a preacher, justifying what they had done. I have never taken well to preaching. I am a very independent thinker, so being preached to by a kidnapper was not on my list of things to hear, before I die. I also don't condone hitting women, but if I could have, I would have liked to "bitch-slap" some sense into her.

Our thirty-minute visit ended with her saying, "Not to worry about me, my suffering is for Jesus, and he will save me from prison, and soon I'll be playing music for God." I pictured a long-haired hippy, in a robe, pulling up to the jail in a beat up truck; wrapping a chain around the bars and busting her out of there. With that thought, I smiled at her and left the jail.

Her defense lawyers called me a few weeks later and asked if I would help with the defense. I told them, "I don't have anything good to say about Wanda, so I really can't help."

They said "It was not about having something good to say, but about helping her get the help she needs."

I stood firm in my decision not to help Wanda, and her lawyers haven't contacted me since. My feelings are of abandonment by Wanda of my siblings and me, so maybe I am using this opportunity to abandon her. As far as Brian goes, I think the World would be a better place if they could figure out a way to bring him to justice, but I can't think of any humanitarian way to do that, so I guess I will settle on the many inhumane thoughts I have like; wrapping bacon around his testicles and letting rabid dogs loose on him, for now. That may sound hypocritical to some people. After all, I was not a very good person for the majority of my life, but I never kidnapped or molested a child either, and in my book that is one of the worst things a person can do. Children are the most innocent creatures in the World, and to kill that innocence in a child is right along the lines of murdering someone, in my opinion.

I feel fortunate for my life right now. By all accounts I should have been in prison for several stupid decisions in my life. I was definitely a product of my environment, and through my co-dependant nature, a victim to the rest of the World. I always used my upbringing as an excuse to act whatever way I wanted, and everybody else was just going to have to deal with it. I could not have been more wrong in my assumption, and it was sweet relief for me to finally come to this conclusion. With the goal I made, and still continue to have, I thought that money was going to solve my problems. Thanks to the widely known stupidity of at least one of my parents, I chose to search myself, and discover who I truly am. This made me realize that money was not a measure of success, but, instead a by-product of good judgment. **I now find myself helping people instead of hurting them and instilling this belief wherever I can.**

God has nothing to do with my life, and he never will. I am okay with that fact, and I find more peace without him than with him. This may be "shocking" to some, and "piss others off", but my life experiences and knowledge steer me away from him. This is not a bad thing, nor does it make me a bad person. It instead, makes me an individual, and this life mine.

People search for their own existence, their own reality; if we are created in "God's" image, what image is he? With so many religions and several different cultures, who is right? What do we believe as our lives pass by in the blink of a cosmic eye? Truthfully, nobody can say for sure, but some people will instill a belief into anyone who is willing to accept it, and accepting something is a personal choice. Some people think they can act in any manner they see fit, as long as they repent on Sunday.

I believe that our lives are not about our "afterlives". Our lives are about our time on Earth, here and now. It is about our families, our daily activities, how we behave in our communities, and interact with our fellow man, that shall ultimately decide our fate as a life form on this planet. What will you leave behind when your time has come; something good for future generations - or havoc for a modern World?

At the fairly young age of thirty-five, my life has come full circle, and I have finally evolved into a good man and a successful human being. I am very thankful for this, and now I always look forward to a new day. **When my time here comes to an end, I cannot say, but when it does, I will die with a smile and know I did my best.**

About the Author

Derrick is a 35 year old male, with many notches under his belt. After a life of torment and pain brought on by his up-bringing, he's come to realize there's more to life. The "more" comes from wanting to help people in his community with honesty, decency and individuality. Derrick is the middle child of Wanda Barzee, and the step-son of Brian David Mitchell, (the two people accused of kidnapping Elizabeth Smart).

A college graduate in 2004, from the "Utah School of Computer Imaging;" Derrick's goal is to ultimately work in the film industry. After teaming up with two schoolmates, he finished a screenplay for a 3D animated movie. Also, Derrick uses his knowledge of computer graphics to illustrate children's books he's written.